Praise for Meditation with Intention

"Anusha Wijeyakumar skillfully presents an authentic, accessible approach to yogic wisdom practices that is grounded in her upbringing, nourished by her own self-care, and informed by her experiences as a meditation teacher and life coach. Wijeyakumar's heartfelt passion, clarity of language, and valuable perspective as a woman of the South Asian diaspora offer a transformational message of peace and purpose for all of us."

—Rashmi Bismark, MD, MPH, preventive medicine physician, yoga and mindfulness teacher, and author of *Finding Om*

"Anusha's practical approach to living with intention makes mindfulness and heartfulness accessible to anyone with the courage to pick up this book. As a step-by-step guide to living a balanced, more peaceful life, these pages hold wisdom for beginners and advanced practitioners alike. By demystifying meditation, Anusha sets a positive ripple in the pond we all share as home. Do yourself a favor and give it a try. You will not regret it."

—Robert G. Louis, MD, FAANS, director of the Skull Base and Pituitary Tumor Program, Pickup Family Neurosciences Institute and director of XR Development at Hoag Memorial Hospital

"For women unfamiliar with mindfulness practices, meditation can be intimidating, but not with Anusha as a guide. As she says, let's all bring meditation down from the mountaintop and incorporate it into daily life! Meditation reduces anxiety and depression, helps us manage pain, and makes us healthier and more resilient. Everyone can adopt a daily meditation practice through the accessible wisdom she shares in this book."

—Heather R. Macdonald, MD, medical director of the High Risk Breast & Ovarian Cancer Program at Hoag Memorial Hospital and assistant clinical professor at USC Keck School of Medicine

"As a human-resources professional, we find ourselves supporting and guiding our clients through challenges an
be truly effective unless we are taking c

spirit. Anusha's message was not only positive, but enabled us to start thinking about the concrete, tangible actions we all could take to refocus and be present. She is a gifted speaker and thinker. Her theories are solidly grounded science and reflect the real-life matrix of personal and professional conflicts and the resolutions they demand."

—Ramona H. Agrela, MPA, CCP, SHRM,associate chancellor/chief human resources executive at the University of California, Irvine

"As an interventional cardiologist taking care of patients with heart attacks, I am a huge proponent of prevention strategies. I believe what Anusha can teach us about mindfulness and meditation can help us reduce stress and anxiety and help increase our focus on good health and boost our overall sense of happiness."

—Dipti Itchhaporia, MD, FACC, FAHA, FESC, vice president of American College of Cardiology and Eric & Sheila Samson Endowed Chair in Cardiovascular Health, director of disease management at Hoag Memorial Hospital

"The seemingly magical but straightforward solutions outlined in this book are tried and true to provide clarity for self-management and mental accountability, no matter the situation. I highly recommend this book to add to your library of accessible solution-based resources to change your life in only five minutes a day."

—Janessa Mondestin, MBA, C-IAYT yoga therapist, E-RYT 500, YACEP, director of People & Culture, Yoga International, and founder of Soulthentic Yoga, RYS 300 School

"I love how Anusha's book reveals meditation as simple practices that can become a 24-7-365 affair of our heart. Profound and practical, this seminal work reveals practices we can easily embody to nourish unshakable well-being and peace amidst the daily challenges of our lives. A must-read!"

—Richard Miller, PhD, founder of iRest Meditation and author of *iRest Meditation*

"Anusha brings a wide scope of expertise to her work and teachings. Based on her upbringing in the Hindu tradition, she was able to blend the foundations of yoga with the core teachings of mindfulness. Her work is so very needed in the world today as we navigate these changing times. The world is a better place because Anusha said 'YES' to her calling; that calling and this book have the capacity to impact many."

—Flossie Park, E-RYT 500, YACEP, yoga teacher & wellness presenter, director of the 200-hour Gentle & Hatha Yoga Teacher Trainings–Soul of Yoga, Encinitas, California

"I used to find the concept of meditation foreign and intimidating, but Anusha's approach to mindfulness is practical, logical, and evidence based…anyone can do it! As a physician, I appreciate the tremendous value of mindfulness and meditation in achieving and maintaining good health, both mental and physical. Do yourself a favor and read this book!"

—January Lopez, MD, medical director of breast imaging at Hoag Memorial Hospital and assistant clinical professor at USC Keck School of Medicine

"I am thrilled that Anusha has put some of her profound teachings into this book that invites so many more people to see the massive impact that sitting in silence can have on every level of our lives…even in just five minutes. This book is a gift and is sure to shift the collective consciousness towards justice, peace, and compassion."

—Jamie Hanson, MEd, E-RYT 500, E-RPYT, founder and lead teacher of the Empowered Yoga Teacher Training™, faculty and board member for Embody Love Movement®

"These potent and accessible meditation practices are designed for *everyone* and *anyone*. And when people can create peace within themselves, they are more capable and equipped to create peace outside themselves. As such, *Meditation with Intention* is a gift to humanity."

—Melanie Klein, empowerment coach, professor of sociology and gender/women's studies, cofounder of the Yoga & Body Image Coalition and coeditor of *Yoga & Body Image*

"Steeped in the Indian Vedic tradition, Anusha Wijeyakumar is an authentic voice in the world of Yoga and Meditation, who LIVES and EMBODIES her practice. I absolutely love her short yet very effective monthly meditations and affirmations, and frequently recommend them to my Ayurveda clients. And now we are lucky to have this gem of a book on meditation from her that will benefit so many more people to find pockets of peace and tranquility in the midst of their busy and stressful lives."

—Sandhiya Ramaswamy, AD, PKS, CMT, MBA, Ayurveda wellness coach & spiritual mentor at Alchemy Ayurveda

"Through her compassionate and inspiring platform, Anusha Wijeyakumar shares a compelling mixture of wisdom and peace. And now, she has found a way to make meditation both accessible and enjoyable. In the midst of such uncertain times, Wijeyakumar has given us what we all need more than ever: peace, stillness, and a way to return to ourselves."

—Saumya Dave, MD, psychiatrist, cofounder of thisisforHER and author of *Well-Behaved Indian Women*

"*Meditation with Intention* represents the next step in the evolution of the sacred teachings on yoga and meditation. We are being offered instruction that is both authentic and accessible—a special combination that has been hard to come by in the recent past. Wijeyakumar has given us the most sacred of all gifts, a kind and gentle introduction to the life-changing practice of meditation, and I'm extremely grateful. She connects the dots between the sacred texts and our modern practice in a way that will be so useful for a new generation of meditators."

—Jivana Heyman, C-IAYT, E-RYT500, founder of Accessible Yoga

MEDITATION
with
INTENTION

About the Author

Anusha Wijeyakumar, MA is a sought-after motivational speaker around the world on the science of mindfulness and meditation. She has delivered keynote speeches for executives at Fortune 500 companies and top-ranked universities across North America and the UK. Anusha is the Wellness Consultant for Hoag Hospital, one of the leading hospitals in the US, where she is actively engaged in championing mindfulness and meditation practices for maternal mental health programs, early risk assessment for breast and ovarian cancer prevention programs, and breast cancer survivorship programs. Anusha is one of the first people to create a meditation program used in clinical research at Hoag Hospital. Anusha is a board member of MOMS Orange County, and she cofounded the movement Womxn of Color + Wellness, both of which focus on increasing diversity, inclusion, and accessibility in the yoga, mindfulness, and wellness communities.

Quick & Easy Ways to
Create Lasting Peace

MEDITATION with INTENTION

LLEWELLYN PUBLICATIONS
WOODBURY, MINNESOTA

First Edition
Third Printing, 2023

Cover design by Kevin R. Brown
Interior art by Mary Ann Zapalac

Library of Congress Cataloging-in-Publication Data
Names: Wijeyakumar, Anusha, author.
Title: Meditation with intention : quick & easy ways to create lasting peace / Anusha Wijeyakumar, MA.
Description: First edition. | Woodbury, Minnesota : Llewellyn Publications, 2020. | Includes bibliographical references. | Summary: "Guide to beginning a daily meditation practice; includes exercises and guided meditations. Secular practices but author's knowledge is Hindu/Buddhist"— Provided by publisher.
Identifiers: LCCN 2020041253 (print) | LCCN 2020041254 (ebook) | ISBN 9780738762685 (paperback) | ISBN 9780738762968 (ebook)
Subjects: LCSH: Meditation.
Classification: LCC BL627 .W493 2020 (print) | LCC BL627 (ebook) | DDC 204/.35—dc23
LC record available at https://lccn.loc.gov/2020041253
LC ebook record available at https://lccn.loc.gov/2020041254

Llewellyn Publications
A Division of Llewellyn Worldwide Ltd.
2143 Wooddale Drive
Woodbury, MN 55125-2989
www.llewellyn.com

Printed in the United States of America

Dedication

This book is dedicated to my parents Wijey and Malathie. I am eternally grateful for your guidance and encouragement in my life. Without your unconditional love, support, and sacrifices I would not be who I am today.

Contents

List of Exercises

Disclaimer

The material in this book is not intended as a substitute for trained medical or psychological advice, or to diagnose, treat, or cure any illness. Readers are advised to consult their personal healthcare professionals regarding treatment and usage. It is the recommendation of both the author and the publisher to use the content herein and its practices with common sense and the advice of trained healthcare professionals.

Foreword

As a breast cancer surgeon, you meet a variety of personalities in your patients and colleagues around the hospital, but few have left such a mark as Anusha Wijeyakumar. We met by chance at a charity event hosted by the hospital where we work and had an instant connection. We found many things in common, including our South Asian heritage, and became fast friends.

After attending a meditation led by Anusha, I realized her work and practice could have a huge impact on the psychosocial well-being of the breast cancer patients I treat.

As the program director of Integrative Breast Oncology at Hoag Hospital, I lead the breast cancer survivorship program that helps women affected by breast cancer live their healthiest life and move past their active cancer diagnosis into thrivorship. Anxiety, PTSD, and depression are just some of the psychosocial issues that impact our patients after going through aggressive surgery, radiation, and chemotherapy treatments. I wondered if mindfulness and meditation could help some of these women move past the stress that may have contributed to their diagnosis in the first place.

I asked Anusha to lead meditations and speak at various survivorship events and immediately received wonderful feedback from patients. Anusha quickly became an integral part of our program and her five-minute quick and easy techniques for mindfulness and meditation have become a hit for breast cancer patients and survivors alike. She has made it easy and fun for our patients to begin a meditation practice, and I am confident this book will help the readers in the same way with her accessible wisdom and simple exercises. I hate to sound cliché, but five minutes a day of meditation and mindfulness is just what the doctor ordered.

Dr. Sadia Khan, FACS
Breast Surgical Oncologist
Director of Integrative Breast Oncology
Hoag Memorial Hospital Presbyterian
Assistant Clinical Professor of Surgery
Keck School of Medicine
The University of Southern California

Introduction

Just like most people in the world, I struggled to gain control of my negative internal chatter for many years. It's amazing how much time you can spend attempting to be in control of your thoughts, often feeling that there may be no end in sight! Through the ancient practices of meditation, yoga, and mindfulness, I have been able to achieve a semblance of inner peace, along with many other blessings in my life. You too can find inner peace and a deeper meaning in your life through the simple wisdom, intentions, and exercises outlined in this book.

If you have five minutes to spare in your day—and let's be honest you do, we all do—this book will help you on your path toward finding more focus and balance in your life. You will learn through the tangible tools and simple exercises I outline how to dial down that constant internal negative narrative and turn up the volume of your true positive inner essence. My favorite saying I have coined over the years is the wallpaper of your mind becomes the landscape of your life. Join me on this journey toward revolutionizing your mind to transform your life.

I am not claiming to be a guru or a yoga master. I am also not proclaiming to be an "expert" at meditation or mindfulness. I am simply sharing what I have learned in my own personal practice and in my professional life. As the daughter of Sri Lankan Tamil Hindu immigrants, this book marries East and West together and was inspired by my own experiences with meditation, yoga, and mindfulness over the years.

I was born and raised in the philosophy of Sanatana Dharma, or Hinduism as it is more widely referred to post colonialism. *Sanatana* means eternal and *dharma* means duty or path of right conduct. This eternal spiritual path has made up the fabric of my life since birth. I have also studied Hinduism and Buddhism formally under a number of different lineages around the world over the past three decades. These practices have made me the woman I am, and it is a blessing to be able to spread this ancestral wisdom instilled in me by my family to the world.

Writing this book is especially meaningful to me as there has been so much cultural appropriation of yoga and meditation in the West with such few works written by authors who are south Asian and Hindu, and in particular female authors. It is wonderful to see that we are in a time now where authenticity and representation matters. We are experiencing a shifting tide where people want to hear from genuine voices they can resonate with, relate to, and learn from in an authentic way.

In today's political and cultural climate, authenticity, inclusivity, and diverse voices are what needs more representation in this genre in particular. Yoga and meditation are lived experiences that are not just about saying the right things but much more importantly about actually doing them. Having this knowledge from childhood as a foundation is vital to me in spreading the true message of these practices in an authentic and inclusive way.

In my professional life as a clinician, I have utilized my lifelong study of the practices of meditation and mindfulness to pioneer a meditation program, currently being used in clinical research at Hoag Hospital in Orange County, California, one of the leading hospitals in the United States. The program I created for this study explores the use of meditation and pranayama breath work in reducing perioperative pain and distress in newly diagnosed breast cancer patients. We are tracking use of narcotic pain medication postoperatively as opioid addiction has become an epidemic in the US. We will also be exploring continuation of a regular meditation practice after the acute surgical period as a way to reduce anxiety, fatigue, and depression.

In addition, I am a professional speaker around the world on the science of meditation and mindfulness. I am also the wellness consultant for Hoag Hospital, where I lead the mindfulness and meditation initiatives for their Women's Health Institute. I am actively involved in their maternal mental health program, breast cancer survivorship, and breast and ovarian high-risk cancer prevention program. I am a certified yoga and meditation teacher alongside being a certified professional life coach with a private practice.

Meditation changes lives and I have witnessed this firsthand with my patients and clients who have struggled with a multitude of mental health issues, including depression, anxiety, as well as alcohol and drug addiction. I have also seen the impact of meditation and mindfulness on women I have worked with battling breast and ovarian cancer. Bringing the ancient wisdom of my ancestral practices to these clinical programs and my own private practice brings me great joy as I am very passionate about empowering people to lead their best lives.

My main goal is to inspire others by sharing what has worked for my patients, clients, and myself through the power of meditation and mindfulness. These practices have certainly aided me on my journey with feeling more love, compassion, and nonjudgment toward others and myself, and isn't this what life is about after all? Breaking down our own barriers within to create more joy and peace in our lives, and then being able to spread this love to others in an authentic way. The good news is that these practices are available to everybody and all it takes is just five minutes a day.

Nobody can honestly tell me that they don't have five minutes. We spend far more than five minutes scrolling through social media, watching YouTube videos, or just filling our time with endless conversations, mindless television, and reading the tabloids. Those things all have their purpose and we all do them and enjoy it, but again we have five minutes to spend in a mindfulness or meditation practice alongside doing all of the other things that we find the time to do in our day, especially when this five-minute practice can and will transform your life.

I can guarantee you that spending five minutes scrolling through your social media feed or looking at cat memes will not have this impact. Don't get me wrong, I love an animal meme as much as the next person, but if you have time to look at cat memes you also have five minutes to spend in your day doing something that will lead you toward a happier and more fulfilled life.

This book is offered as a source of knowledge and wisdom to my readers and the wider community, on how you can bring ancient Eastern wisdom to life in a modern world and transform your mind and life to find lasting peace from within. So if, no matter what you do, you can't seem to slow down your mind, stay present, relax, or go to sleep without the aid of multiple glasses of wine or sleep aids, then this book is for you.

In this book, I offer simple accessible tools to help you develop and commit to a daily mindfulness and meditation practice that will assist you on your journey toward creating peace and happiness from within. Each chapter has a specific intention and five-minute exercise associated with it. The intention set at the outset of each chapter is the theme that you should carry with you as you move throughout reading the chapter. Each intention is tied to the simple five-minute exercise that concludes the chapters. The exercise outlined at the end of each chapter will enable you to start fully living in the present moment by becoming unchained from your past and cease worrying about the future.

You can revisit the intentions and five-minute exercises as often as you wish; the more you do them, the easier it will become to incorporate them into your daily life. Through dedicated commitment and effort comes change. May the words in this book have as much meaning and significance to you as they do for me and aid you on your journey toward creating lasting transformation from within. We all deserve inner peace, self-love, and self-acceptance in order to be our best selves and find a deeper purpose in our lives.

Warmly,
Anusha

Intention 1

I change my mindset to change my life

Meditation is a word that can conjure images of lotus pose and sitting in silence for long periods of time, which quite frankly is not accessible to most of us nor seems like much fun. I mean, who wants to choose to sit alone with their thoughts and worries to only end up feeling more stressed than before? Part of changing our mindset about meditation is understanding why we should even meditate at all. Why is it worth it?

Even if you are aware of the benefits of having a daily meditation practice in your life, it can feel very daunting and inaccessible. The things we'll explore in this chapter will help shift your perception to be more open by learning the roots of the practice and how meditation shapes your mind and brain. You will also be equipped to start a simple daily meditation practice in three easy and accessible steps.

We have read about meditating, thought about meditating, and even for a lot of us actually tried to sit down and meditate but often without achieving what we had hoped for. The number one complaint that I receive from my clients and patients is that they have tried meditation before but it just does not seem to work for them. We all lead busy lives, and the thought of sitting silently for thirty minutes each day with our monkey mind does not seem feasible or enjoyable!

Being born and raised as a Hindu, the path of yoga and meditation, which is one of the six schools of Hindu philosophy that originated in India, has made up the fabric of my life. I remember going to prayers with my mother from childhood. There was a period where the lights down would be turned down and there was a set time to meditate after the bhajan (a form of devotional call-and-response singing) was over, before the chanting of mantras. This was one of my favorite times as the room would be so still and silent and there was a real sense of peace and unity within and all around me as I felt that I was connecting back to the divine. This is the true essence of what yoga and meditation is all about.

Meditation and Medication

On a basic level, meditation practices help calm an overactive brain that if left unmanaged, can lead to anxiety and insomnia. We are fully aware of how much of an issue stress has become in this modern age as we live in such a fast-paced society with never-ending to-do lists. Stress and anxiety affect us all physically, emotionally, and mentally and have become a leading cause in the spread of disease.

There is an increasing reliance on prescription medicine to deal with a lot of these symptoms, and I see this firsthand with the work I am engaged in with patients in drug and alcohol addiction treatment centers. Unfortunately, this reliance often leads to the symptom being treated but *not* the root cause. It is only when we begin the journey into the mind to deal with what is really causing the anxiety, insomnia, or depression that we are able to get to the root of the issue, work on releasing this pain, and heal ourselves from within.

I must add that meditation is not the answer to suddenly come off your medication and go cold turkey with the hope that meditation and mindfulness will solve all of your mental health problems. I have had patients and clients with long histories of depression and high levels of anxiety whom I encouraged to stay on their medications or sometimes even seek out medical assistance to find a suitable medication to help alleviate their immediate suffering. In addition to their medications, they adopt and commit to a daily meditation practice, which will no doubt help.

For some people with a dedicated meditation practice, they have been able to successfully reduce their dosage or come off their medication completely with the blessing of their medical doctor. Again, meditation is *your* practice, so it doesn't matter what anyone else is doing or saying. There is no one right way to meditate and of course you can still meditate while on medication and feel the power of the practice. Holistic wellness practices such as yoga, meditation, and mindfulness that focus on integrative medicine are wonderful complements to medication and have helped countless people manage their depression and anxiety more effectively.

Meditation and Your Mind

The benefits to meditating regularly are scientifically proven and are of course endless. After all, who does not want peace of mind and inner sanctity in the craziness and constant whirlwind of activity that surrounds us? Science also verifies that cultivating compassion and mindful awareness in our lives by living in the present enables us to transform our relationship with ourselves and become our own best friend. In reality, other people liking you is a bonus; you liking and accepting yourself is the real prize and goal toward which we should all be working.

It all sounds so good in theory. Who doesn't want to calm down the monkey mind and have some inner peace amid all of that constant inner chatter and be their own best friend instead of their own worst enemy. The truth of the matter is that a regular meditation practice is going to bring you closer to this goal of becoming your own best friend and will also help in finding and maintaining that elusive inner peace.

Committing to a regular dedicated meditation practice seems the most difficult part to attain and stick to for many people. The results you are seeking will simply not come without having the discipline to commit to a daily practice. It is the discipline and focus that one needs to cultivate from within first in order to make that commitment to making meditation a daily part of your life. Once you do you realize that meditation helps you to befriend yourself. If you can learn to be our own best friend in life, you are choosing a path filled with greater self-love and self-acceptance. This is a far more preferable path than living with the harsh inner critic and constantly judging yourself and others in a negative cycle that seems never ending.

My meditation practice has allowed me to release the past and not fixate on the future, but to instead learn to trust the process and surrender to a higher power that I feel guides me forward on my path. Whether you believe in a higher power or not, meditation is a process of liberating ourselves from our own bondage within, and that bondage is our mind and ego.

In yoga philosophy, the mind has four aspects. The first is *manas,* the mind itself, or the thinking faculty of the mind. The second is the *buddhi,* the intellect or the mind's will power. The third is the *ahamkara*, or the ego aspect, and the fourth is the *chitta,* the substance through which the faculties of the mind operate. The ego is ever ready to deter us from our path of meditation, which is why as soon as you try to come into a place of stillness and quiet, some body part will start itching or hurting, willing you to move or scratch the itch.

Yoga is an ancient science of the mind that affords you the ability to stop those fluctuating ripples in the mind from occurring through dedicated practice. As a result, you will be able to see the reflection of your true essence within this still reflection without all the ripples and waves that make our own beauty and divine essence so difficult to see. Part of the journey with meditation is understanding that first we must bring the mind under our control by withdrawing the senses and gaining mastery over the physical body.

We call this in yoga philosophy *pratyahara* or withdrawal of the senses. *Pratyahara* is the fifth limb on Patanjali's eight-limb path of yoga detailed in Patanjali's *Yoga Sutra*, the ancient sacred Hindu text on yoga written in approximately 200 CE. The *Yoga Sutra* is the ultimate book on yoga philosophy and provides students of yoga and meditation with all they need to develop and maintain a practice. You will come to learn this is one of my all-time favorite books by how often I refer to it! The eight-limbed path of yoga as detailed by Patanjali, who was a scientist and yoga master, was that yoga and meditation is a science of the mind and a path in which to control the fluctuations of the mind.

The journey of meditation is also all about controlling the ego or the *ahamkara* as it is called in Sanskrit and yoga philosophy. What I like to call the small "i" that we so often associate with ourselves. Through yoga and meditation, we are able to remember that we are in fact the big "I." By doing so, we become empowered to stop sweating all the little things and actually start embracing our power within to live up to our full potential in this life. We learn to trust and surrender on our path in life and have full faith that the divine plan for ourselves is unfolding exactly as it should.

Meditation and Your Brain

Part of committing to a daily meditation practice enables you to actually affect your brain function resulting in better emotional and mental health. Even though research into meditation and its effects is still in its infancy, studies have illustrated that meditation helps to suppress the amygdala, which is the jumpy part of our brain that results in us constantly living in that state of fight or flight. It's like the alarm system always going off in your home for no good reason.

The brain is the primary shaper of your mind and in turn your reality. It is always working and uses about the same amount of energy whether you are fast asleep or wide awake. It never gets a break and even though it only makes up two percent of the body's weight, it uses twenty-five percent of the body's oxygen and glucose and fifteen percent of the body's cardiac output. Meditation is a wonderful way to give your brain and mind a much-needed time-out and go to that place of peace within.

Becoming Less Reactionary

Meditation will change your life and only for the better, I guarantee it. It will enable you to become less reactionary to everyday situations and start creating a place of balance and equanimity from within. When your triggers are pushed, which inevitably they will be, through these practices you can come back to your place of balance and peace within.

We always want other people to change. I can't remember the amount of times as it happens so often when I have heard from my clients and patients how much they want their partner, or their children, or colleagues to change. I always tell them that change happens when *we* change. Once we change, our perception of things shifts and our reaction to things is different and everything transforms around us.

Meditation and mindfulness practices enable us to feel love, compassion and nonjudgment toward others and ourselves, which are key aspects of a self-love and self-care practice. This makes us less reactive to other people and our external circumstances, which is life altering. Who doesn't want to feel more love authentically for themselves and others?

My meditation and mindfulness practice has changed my life beyond measure. It has given me the gift of liberating myself from the prison of my own mind and allowed me to embrace the beauty of the present moment and live my life each day more fully with greater awareness and love. This has also empowered me to let go of trying to control everyone and everything around me and learn to sit back and enjoy the journey more, which has been a liberating experience for a control freak like myself!

The more we are able to let go in our lives the more peace we feel from within. Ironically, we are then much more able to attract the things we want effortlessly. Once I learned to let go and allowed the divine to guide me, the more joy I feel in my daily life and the more opportunities come to me without forcing them and trying to control everyone and everything in my life, which I might add becomes exhausting.

Beginning a Meditation Practice

To change your mindset away from the assumption that meditation has to be hard, let's explore how you can begin a meditation practice easily. In all honesty, if it the method is not simple and accessible, you are not going to do it, which is a common stumbling block. We will look at this in two easy steps.

1. An effective and uncomplicated way to begin is by making a commitment to remain in stillness during your meditation. What this could translate to as you begin a practice is not moving or opening your eyes and using your powers of concentration to overpower any instincts that are trying to distract you from this inner focus and awareness.

   When teaching a meditation class or workshop, I often notice that people can't help but open their eyes and look around the room to see what everybody else is doing rather than focusing on what they are supposed to be doing. After opening their eyes mid-practice, these people are then overcome by panic upon seeing that everybody else is doing the practice and they are the only ones who aren't. From there, the self-doubt and self-judgment kick in, and they forget why they are there in the first place! I am sure many of you can relate to this as you begin a practice; we've all been there. Just focus on stillness and trust it.
2. Ensure that the spine is straight. That's it—you don't need to be sitting with the tongue on the roof of your mouth staring at the tip of your nose unless you wish to, nor must you twist into any acrobatic positions. Simply make sure that

whether you are sitting in a chair or on the floor or lying down that the spine including the cervical spine is in a straight line. There is a very valid reason for this: according to the ancient yogis, there are three principal nadis or nerve currents along the spine that we focus on in a meditation and pranayama or breath work practice. With that in mind, let's look more at what the nadis and energy centers are all about.

Purposeful Position: Chakras and Nadis

Looking at the chakras and nadis will help you understand that there is purpose to how we position ourselves in meditation. The nadi or nerve current on the left is called *ida*, which is the feminine lunar energy. The nadi on the right is the *pingala* or masculine solar energy, and the center column through the spine is the *sushumna nadi* where the seven chakras are located. *Chakra* is the Sanskrit word for "wheel," and in the practice of yoga and meditation, there are seven wheels or what are commonly referred to as energy centers in the body located along the spine. These energy centers begin at the base of the spine and ascend all the way up to the crown of the head.

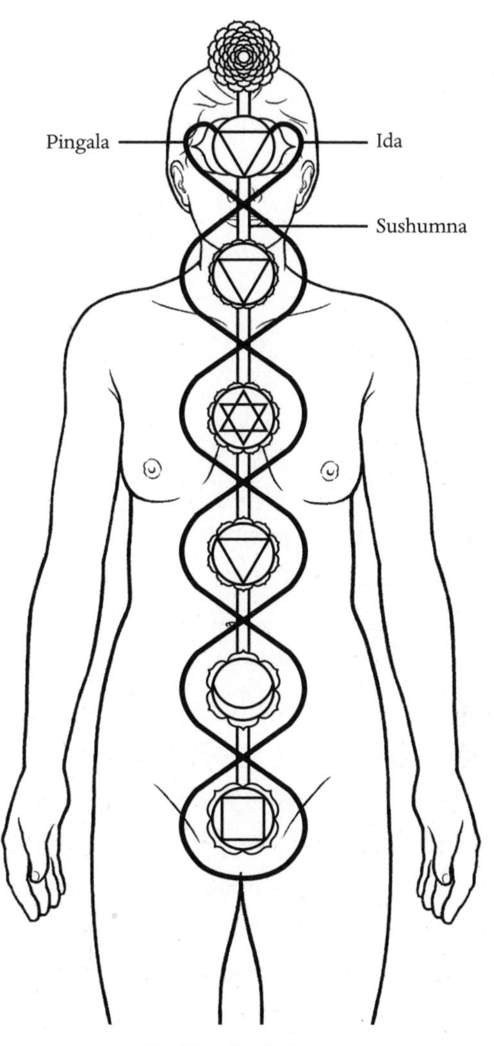

Ida, Pingala, Sushumna

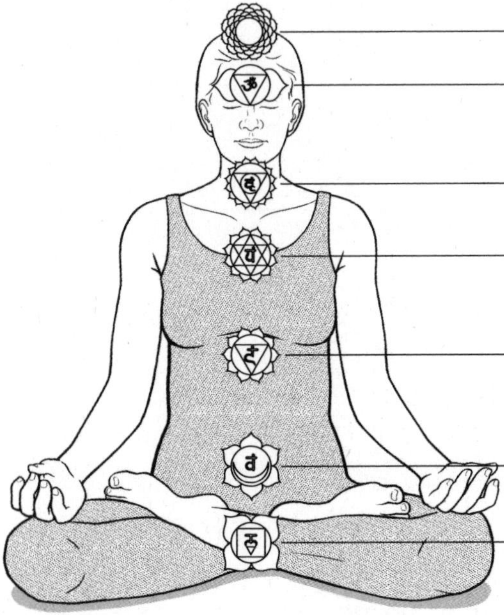

Sahasrara
Crown Chakra

Ajna
Third Eye Chakra

Vishuddha
Throat Chakra

Anahata
Heart Chakra

Manipura
Solar Plexus Chakra

Svadhishthana
Sacral Chakra

Muladhara
Root Chakra

Chakras

Currents are constantly going through both the ida and pingala nadis, but the sushumna nadi is closed and can only be opened through deep concentration and dedication to the practice of yoga and meditation. The sole purpose of opening the sushumna nadi is the gaining enlightenment and the merging of our individual consciousness with universal consciousness, which is what the path of yoga and meditation is all about. It is also why sitting up straight or lying down flat and having the spine in a neutral position with the head and neck in one straight line is such an important part of a meditation and pranayama breath work practice.

Meditation means that the mind is able to be turned on itself. There are three stages in a meditation practice that are detailed in Patanjali's *Yoga Sutra* and the eight-limbed path of yoga covered earlier in this chapter. The first is *dharana*, the sixth limb, which is the ability to concentrate the mind upon any object and therefore bring the mind under your control. The next is *dhyana*, the seventh limb that is the state of entering meditation. If you are not able to master the art of concentration, you will never be able to get to this limb, which is a state of deep meditation. Concentration is key to a successful meditation practice and quite frankly to getting anything done successfully in life!

By gaining control of the subconscious mind you gain control over the conscious. The eighth and final limb is *samadhi*, the end goal of a yogi or person truly committed to the path of yoga and meditation. In this state, the mind becomes fully absorbed in divine and universal consciousness. It may sound like a lofty goal to most of us, but we see the benefits of a daily yoga and meditation practice with continued dedication.

Shifting Judgment

Now let's look at changing our mindset about judgments we may have about superficial presentations of meditation. The appropriation of yoga and meditation in the West is real and can be quite offensive to somebody like myself who was born and raised as a Hindu, especially in California where it seems to have taken on a life of its own, and not in a good way. I think what so often turns people off of yoga is the commercialization and commoditization of a spiritual discipline that tends to focus on what society perceives to be perfect body shapes, with a definite focus on the very thin.

And of course, the majority of people pictured in the mainstream yoga scene are white, able-bodied women and men without a thought to how important diversity, inclusion, and accessibility are in yoga and wellness. Representation and diverse voices are unfortunately missing in a lot of yoga studios, yoga teacher trainings, yoga brands, and wellness environments that focus so much on the physical, the ego, and the showmanship in contrast to what the true essence of yoga is really about—the letting go of the ego.

It is easy to feel frustrated and judge all of this—believe me, I do—but what I try to do as best I can is practice nonjudgment and work on letting go of judgment, as hard as it can be. Anyone who tells you they don't judge is just lying to themselves, as we all do it. The key is to be honest with yourself and bring awareness to your internal judgments so you can focus on releasing them with love and compassion toward yourself and others. This doesn't mean that we ignore things that need to be called out or addressed in society as the path of yoga is to work on putting your practice into action by addressing injustices and inequalities in society. Being silent means we can become complicit to these issues.

There is a danger in removing the spirituality behind these practices; white-washing them, seen so often in the mainstream, means losing the essence and true purpose of a yoga, meditation, and mindfulness practice. We practice to remove our own suffering initially and can then turn our focus toward alleviating the suffering of others. When one of us suffers, we all suffer. In yoga philosophy, the meaning of life is to not just focus on our own happiness but to live our lives with a purpose, to matter, be productive, and have it make some difference that we lived at all, especially in these challenging times.

The message of yoga and meditation has been greatly diluted in the West. The word *yoga* is derived from the

Sanskrit *yuj*, which refers to the union of the individual consciousness with God or universal consciousness. So as a yogi or yogin, a person on the path of yoga, we are yoking all of our thoughts, words, and actions to God, certainly a far cry from the glossy, filtered images on social media of scantily clad, skinny women in yoga postures that feeds into spiritual bypassing and cultural appropriation.

Many people choose to just stay on the physical path of yoga, which is the asana. *Asana* is the third limb of Patanjali's eight-limbed path of yoga, but it is the one on which people in the West are fixated. What people fail to comprehend is that the essence of yoga is all about meditation, which is why the physical practice is done in the first place. To just focus on the physical makes it not yoga—the union of our two selves and individual and universal states of consciousness merging together as one— but something else entirely. You will not get there in a handstand, trust me on this one.

The whole reason we do asana, which are the physical poses and limb three on Patanjali's eight limbed path of yoga as detailed in the *Yoga Sutra,* is in order to ready and steady the mind and body to come to a place of stillness and quiet so you can focus on the real essence of yoga, which is meditation. Through the practices of yoga and meditation, you are able to let go of your limiting thoughts and beliefs and open yourself up to your true nature and the beauty that lies within.

We are never going to change everybody's minds, and with the advent of beer yoga and goat yoga we seem to be losing our way even further from the roots of these practices. I am unclear as to why the word *yoga* is even used in these instances as neither of these things have anything to do with yoga. These are not classes I would personally take or recommend as it goes against the reason I come to my mat and the philosophy of yoga, which is to journey inward without the need or use of external stimulants or stimuli.

While I do yoga as my sole form of physical exercise apart from hiking, in truth I do it much more for mental exercise. As mentioned earlier, yoga is far more than the physical asanas, which just scratch the surface. I would therefore be very skeptical of anyone calling themselves a "master" of yoga and meditation, as that is the exact opposite of what a yoga and meditation practice is all about! Advanced yogis such as Swami Paramahansa Yogananda and Swami Vivekananda never referred to themselves as masters, nor did they claim to have all of life's answers.

Meditation as a Reminder

One of my favorite things to do as part of my job is teach meditation, mindfulness, and breath work practices to people in recovery for serious drug and alcohol addiction. Teaching these groups always gives me so much personal joy. I was teaching a class focused on the throat chakra, the fifth chakra in the body. This is the seat of our voice, center of truth, and the ability to know and express our internal truths to the world around us.

In one group, we completed our first meditation and it was time for sharing stories. One of the clients expressed how the first meditation had reminded him of "who he really is" and how much peace that gave him alongside a sense of powerfulness. The path of yoga and meditation is all about remembering who we really are and uniting with that force within, called the *atman* or soul in yoga philosophy.

The man's statement made my heart smile, as we often forget who we really are because we are chained to our pasts and play the same tape over and over again in our minds, or we worry about the future. The journey with meditation and mindfulness practices reminds us again of what we had once forgotten, that we are all sparks of the divine and it is only through silence that we are able to realize this truth. Patanjali's *Yoga Sutra* mentions only being able to know spirit through silence and the process of tuning into the power of the universe. It always amazes me to see how these practices can transform people so quickly and allow us all the much-needed respite from the busyness and chaos of our own minds. It is like a true tonic for the mind and soul.

If more of the world was meditating, I am convinced we would not see all of the problems that we do today, as so much of it stems from hatred and fear of others different from ourselves that feeds into a fear-based consciousness. Meditation teaches us that we are all one and part of the same universal divine consciousness. The practice allows us to see and really feel that unity among us and in turn learn to extend our love and compassion to all of those around us, not just our friends and family.

Using our power and privilege to alleviate the suffering of others is what the path of meditation is all about. If we are not doing this as part of our meditation and mindfulness practice, it can become futile as we are still only focused on ourselves and our individual self and ego. Saying "we are all on"—a very popularized term in yoga and meditation classes in the West—but then not doing anything to actually effect that change in society is not the path of yoga. Meditation, which is yoga, is a call to action for the soul and a call to right social, moral and economic injustices that we see so prevalent in the world around us.

The more love we can fill our hearts and minds with the more we are able to authentically spread this love to others and live happier and healthier lives while uplifting those around us. If you want more love, give more love; if you want more peace, find more acceptance within. If you want to put meditation into action, engage in service by working toward alleviating the suffering and pain of those marginalized and in need of our help, support and compassion.

True joy lies in service to others. Meditation is a journey of learning to embrace yourself and become your own best friend through self-love and self-acceptance. Once you do this, you naturally want to help uplift those around you. A meditation and mindfulness practitioner is focused on returning to love and letting go of all of the blockages that stop us from seeing our true selves and that divine spark within and around us in all of humanity.

Finding Inner Peace

Inner peace and happiness must come from within in order to be lasting rather than fleeting "feel good" moments. Quite often, I hear people say that they believe meditation is not for them because they can't slow their minds down. My response is that is exactly why we meditate! None of us can slow our minds down, which is why these ancient practices are having such a popular resurgence. People are in dire need of tools to help them slow down, power down, and create some calm.

Meditation allows me to have much more control over my thoughts and myself. When a negative thought enters my mind, I am much more able to redirect it and not chase it down the rabbit hole. We are all fully aware of how tiresome that endless hole is, after all. If you can make a commitment to set aside just five minutes each morning to engage in a meditation practice (preferably) as soon as you have risen, you will find that it sets you up in the best way for the day ahead; you will not be disappointed.

If you can dedicate yourself to following the simple steps outlined below and sit in silence for at least five minutes a day, I guarantee that you will start to feel lighter and brighter. You will be surprised what comes to you from these moments of silence, so make a commitment to yourself, your health, and well-being. Start meditating your way to a new mindset.

Exercise

Five-Minute Morning Meditation

Step 1: You could start by lighting a relaxing scented candle or burning some essential oil in a diffuser to cleanse your space and omit a sense of peace and well-being in your meditation environment. My favorite essential oils to burn in the morning are Aura Cacia's eucalyptus, rosemary, or sage for an uplifting and cleansing start to the day.

Step 2: Read a paragraph of something uplifting to enlighten your mind, body, and spirit. I read Patanjali's *Yoga Sutra* and focus on one sutra a day. This can help with focusing your mind and setting the tone for your practice.

Step 3: Sit on the floor cross-legged or in a chair with the spine straight. Take three deep breaths initially inhaling deeply through the nose and exhaling through the mouth. Slowly begin to turn your awareness within, focusing your mind on your breath, and then gradually toward inner silence. Drown out all of the other distractions so you are able to hear the valuable messages your inner self has to share with you. If thoughts come into the mind which inevitably they will, focus on remaining unattached and letting each thought come and go like a cloud drifting away in the sky.

Intention 2
I let go of excuses

In this chapter, we will delve into how you can commit to a daily meditation practice by letting go of excuses around time, fear, discipline, and perfection. We will break down simple ways so you can stop finding reasons not to meditate and instead begin to shift that narrative and commit to a daily practice.

Did I find my happily ever after at twenty-five? No, I did not, and not many people do. If you are lucky enough to feel as though you have it all together at that age, that's wonderful. My experience has been that the older I get, the more I realize how much I don't know and still have to learn and grow on my journey. Life humbles us, and age truly is our greatest teacher. I am sure the most enlightened minds that have ever graced our planet would agree with this truth.

It has taken a lot of time and effort to gain control over my mind and thoughts, and of course it is still a daily work in progress. I am not going to lie and make it seem as if I have mastered my mind completely and never have a negative thought or worry. Nor will I claim to be an "expert" or "master"—I am simply sharing with you what has worked for me in my own life and the lives of my patients and clients.

Five minutes of meditation a day changed my life. As a result, I have been able to gain more control over my mind and thought processes in order to change my mindset and in turn change my life. From there, I felt empowered to make the transition toward greater self-love and clarity from within. And in case you were wondering, this was all achieved through the intentions and five-minute exercises shared in the following pages. I have also been greatly inspired by the major transformations that have occurred in the lives of my patients and clients around the world. They all began with committing just five minutes a day to a meditation and mindfulness practice. For those who made the commitment to sticking with the practice, the experience has been incredibly transformative.

You Have Five Minutes to Meditate

It always amazes me to see how the commitment of a daily five-minute meditation and mindfulness practice, which seems so small, has such a powerful and lasting effect. I have witnessed patients previously so dedicated to their daily drinking routine make radical changes to their relationship with alcohol. I have seen the effect that only five minutes of daily meditation has on changing people's relationship to toxic relationships and unhealthy lifestyle habits. When our relationship with ourselves is negative, we do not make positive choices, period.

The name of this section has been my favorite phrase over the past few years. We have to learn to let go of the excuses we make about not having enough time. Time is one of our most precious commodities—you can't bring it back, no matter how much money or resources you have. But on your deathbed, you are not going to recall all of the reasons for why you didn't do the things you wanted to or all of the excuses you made; all you will remember is that your life was unfulfilled. The most common regret of people on their deathbeds is that they wish they'd had the courage to live a life true to themselves honoring their *own* needs and wants, not everybody else's. They had not honored many of their dreams and in their final moments realize that it was due to the poor choices made in the past. They also understand that no one else can be blamed, the most difficult part to accept.

After this, the dying person usually has a profound self-realization—they must come to peace with the fact that in life, they were their own worst enemy. That elusive sense of peace and happiness could not be found within, as they were too busy doing everything else. As they say, hindsight is valuable, and sometimes it is too late to rewind the clock and go back to change things. It is not too late for you, however. Make the choice to spend your time engaged in practices such as meditation and mindfulness so you can find that peace and happiness within.

Finding Five Minutes in Your Day

Now let's explore how you can let go of any lingering excuses and find time in your day to commit to a five-minute meditation. Visualize yourself doing your five-minute practice each morning. Think about setting your alarm five minutes earlier than your normal time. Or perhaps you arrive at work five minutes earlier so you can complete the practice in your car or at your desk before your workday begins.

Alternately, you may take five minutes when you get home, before dinner, or before bed. Whatever the case may be, think about how you can commit to making meditation a daily part of your life and committing right now to when you will find the time to add this five-minute practice into your morning. Once you have completed this visualization, it may be helpful to write down when and where you will be completing your practice and make a decision to commit to doing it from today onward.

Believe in Yourself

Believe that you have the power *today* to start reprogramming your mind away from excuses toward a greater commitment to your happiness and inner peace. My personal mantra has not been "Why me?" but instead "Why *not* me?" You must first believe that you have the power to change your life before inner and outer transformation can really begin Even if the odds are stacked against me and success seems impossible, I have to believe in myself first.

If you are trying to manifest anything in your life—be it a relationship, a baby, or a new job—if at some level you don't believe those things will happen for you due to deep-rooted insecurities, then quite simply they won't. Or they may occur and you get a fleeting glimpse of what things could be like in your life before it all goes upside-down because your self-sabotaging thoughts rear their ugly head and ruin it all.

Many people are unaware of the concept of thought as vibration—all of our thoughts actually have a vibration attached to them, so we therefore have the power to manifest our thoughts, good or bad, into reality. If your thoughts are positive, this power can be a blessing, but it feels like more of a curse if they are mainly negative, as most people's tend to be. Could the constant negative thoughts be the reason you feel as though a dark cloud is hanging over you and bad things just seem to follow you wherever you go? Realize now that your thoughts become your reality. And the great news is that you have the power to control the direction of your thoughts and the flow of your life from negative to positive through meditation and mindfulness.

I work with many breast and ovarian cancer patients, both people with a high risk of developing cancer due to a genetic mutation as well as those fighting cancer, surviving, and thriving. Research shows that people with a more positive outlook to their cancer diagnosis and treatment do much better with chemotherapy and radiation versus those who have a more negative and fatalistic attitude. Our bodies pick up on what we tell it at a cellular level through our thoughts, good or bad, via our unique mind and body connection.

We see on numerous occasions the power of the mind that has healed people from incurable diseases and given people the ability to walk again after being told they would spend the rest of their lives in a wheelchair. There are many other miraculous feats that people have achieved against all odds through mastery of their thoughts and minds. If you heal your mind, you can heal your body and your life. Learning to trust your intuition and be led from within is pivotal to this process, as is finding the strength to not give up when the going gets tough, which it inevitably will. It is staggering to think of how many people give up on themselves and their dreams because of barriers along the way.

You can learn to tune in through meditation and mindfulness and if your instincts are guiding you forward to trust them and not be deterred by any obstacles that cross your path. I have learned more and more over time to become guided from within, and it is amazing how the obstacles are cleared away. Obstacles can also be placed in our way to guide us on a different path, perhaps one we would never have gone down if we hadn't started our journey with meditation in the first place.

Let Go of Fear of Tradition

We must first let go of any fear we may have around embracing traditions and cultures that are different to our own. True beauty lies in diversity, and the wonderful thing about meditation is that even though the practice's roots are in Hinduism, they are nondenominational. No matter what your religious beliefs or faith may be, you can use these practices and build them into your own life. In fact, many of these faiths have a meditative aspect to their prayer practices; they just call it by a different name.

The point of meditation is that we are connecting to a higher source outside of ourselves. You can call this whatever you want or what makes you feel most comfortable, whether that name is God, the universe, light, spirit, source, and so on. Whatever you want to call this higher power is your choice. Don't let that be the deterrent of why you are not meditating. You don't have to put a label on it, you can incorporate meditation and mindfulness into your life in the way that serves you best.

Let Go of Perfection

If you don't meditate because you feel you don't do it "right," let that go. Perfection isn't the goal. Failure is a necessary part of the journey toward success, speak to any super successful person and they will tell you this themselves! You may not succeed the first time you try or the tenth time, and this may even relate to your meditation practice! Making mistakes is part of the journey as without the mistakes that you make along your path and the learning that comes from picking yourself up after you stumble or fall, sometimes falling flat on your face, you don't learn the valuable lessons you need to that make you stronger and more resilient.

If you feel as though you have hit rock bottom, welcome that feeling instead of resisting it. The only way forward is up. We may avoid meditation because we don't want to be reminded of things we are resisting, but meditation and mindfulness help so much on this path because they teach us how to tune in and actually listen to what intuition tells us rather than just drowning out that voice or not trusting it. The more you are able to learn to surrender and actually follow your guidance from within, the more you are able to realize your truth and let it guide your life, even if everyone around you tells you something different.

Meditation is not about striving for perfection but about embracing our own imperfections with humility, love, and nonjudgment. I am not perfect at these three things all the time, but I am certainly doing much better as a direct result of my meditation and mindfulness practice. It isn't necessary to become a monk to have a meditation practice that works, nor must you experience some tragedy that leads you down a path of self-realization.

Let Go of the Meditation "Image"

If your excuse not to meditate is that you aren't the right type of person for it, let that go. Meditation is for *everybody*, not just the self-help addict, vegan warrior, and yoga-pant wearing, green juice drinker. If we are honest, this is in fact what turns many people off the practice as they feel they have to look or act a certain way in order to be accepted or for their practice to be taken seriously. Note to self here, reader, your meditation practice is for you! You do not need to justify it or explain it to anybody else. It is your truth and your practice.

I am not a vegetarian; I drink alcohol; and I love handbags, shoes, and lipstick, yet yoga and meditation are still the foundations of my life. It does not mean that I am any less of a practitioner than anybody else, as ultimately what matters is what is in the heart. If you outwardly do all the right things but harbor negativity or ill will toward others, eating a plant-based diet or cycling everywhere won't discount what is going on internally.

The amount of people who do what looks like the right thing to others but fail to do the internal work—which is what's most important—shows that no matter what a person does externally, it still won't shift their internal perspective. The inner peace they crave in life will remain just beyond their reach. What many do not know is that our thoughts shape our lives more than anything else.

Be authentic. Would being vegan help my yoga and meditation practice and the world at large, no doubt it would but I am not ready for that sacrifice just yet. This is something I am seriously working on though and aspire to be as Hinduism espouses vegetarianism and it is a part of our religious practice and belief system. The reason behind it is the concept of *ahimsa* or nonviolence and nonharming as detailed in Patanjali's *Yoga Sutra*. Ahimsa is the first of the *yamas,* which are the ethical codes and universal values related to the path of yoga. Ahimsa is having respect for all living beings and avoidance of violence toward others in thought, word, or action.

Beef has always been off-limits for me, as the cow is considered a sacred animal in Hinduism. Dairy is something I have never liked, so it was easy for me to cut out and use nondairy alternatives as much as possible. What I do is my best and right now that is being plant based for my breakfast and lunch and only eating meat or seafood at dinner. Being honest with yourself and accepting where you are at on your path is also a vital part of a meditation and mindfulness practice. There is no point in pretending you don't eat meat and then shoveling bacon down your throat the first chance you get when you are alone.

People who announce they are vegetarian and then in the same sentence say they eat meat always confused me. Why rush to put a label on yourself? Do it because you want to do it, not because it sounds good or you are trying to live up to the expectations of others, as that is always a recipe for unhappiness and brings us back to the point I made earlier about being authentic and living your best life, not somebody else's version.

You can be many different things without needing to try to be everything to everybody. The path of meditation and mindfulness teaches us to accept ourselves where we are on our journey wherever that may be and to look at our past with love, compassion, and nonjudgment. To learn to fully accept yourself flaws and all that has led you to the place you are at today. To truly make your message authentic, you have to be sincere and that comes from being comfortable in your own skin.

Using the practices of mindfulness in your everyday life will help you become the best version of yourself, not somebody else's best version. Once you become happier with who you are, what anybody else thinks or says starts to become less relevant. Meditation helps you in quieting that inner critic, embracing your strengths and flaws, and gaining the confidence and courage to be who you are truly meant to be in this life. From there, you can go for what you want in accordance with your highest good.

Cultivate Commitment

You are what you do, not what you say you will do. We so often find ourselves saying that we are going to do a lot of things and talk incessantly about doing them without actually making the commitment to ever doing them. We continually make excuses for why we are not doing the things we need to do yet somehow find the time to do the things we want to. I have lost count of how many times I have heard people tell me about how they really want to try meditation. Perhaps they have tried it and know it can help them, but they never seem to find the commitment or resolve to stick to a regular practice because they lack the discipline. Re-read that sentence; as difficult as it may be to swallow, it is the truth.

Discipline is key to success with anything we do in life, and meditation is no different. We need the discipline, motivation, and perseverance to do these practices regularly to feel the benefits. By "regular," I don't mean once every six months. In this book, I will teach you how dedicating just five minutes a day to a meditation practice can and will change your life. I see how life-changing these practices are for people who actually commit to doing them. I am not talking about subtle changes either; I am talking about complete, one-hundred-and-eighty-degree, life-altering changes.

Ultimately, like anything, a mindfulness or meditation practice is not going to work unless you actually *do it*. So often I hear people say that they have been practicing on and off for periods of time but meditation has not worked for them. If you are not able to commit to a dedicated daily practice, you simply will not see the results in your life and that is the cold hard truth.

It is no surprise that meditation has not worked for you if you have only done it five times over the past three years. Like I keep saying throughout this book, we all have five minutes and nobody can honestly tell me they don't have five minutes to spare in their day. Especially when meditation can and will change your life. I see the results in the lives of my patients and clients who adopt meditation and make it an integral part of their daily lives.

The pranayama or breath work meditation provided in chapter 1 is a great place to start a daily practice, only requiring five minutes. I have taken the effort out of it for you. If you don't want to do my meditation, there are countless apps and YouTube videos that will aid you on your journey. Find something that works for you, whether it be what appears in this book, following along with a video or app, or simply sitting in silence for five minutes each day.

Whatever it is you decide to do, make sure you actually do it, as that is the key to success with anything in life. If you don't do the practice, it won't work. View meditation and mindfulness as an essential part of your day, like brushing your teeth, showering, or eating. The more you meditate, the more you realize how much you do miss it if you skip a day and that your life is certainly better with it.

Exercise
Five-Minute Mindfulness Practice

This exercise will help you to commit to a daily mindfulness practice that actually works and it only takes five minutes a day. You gotta love that! Choose to not begin your day with scrolling through endless social media feeds or checking texts and emails immediately upon rising. Instead, devote at least five minutes as soon as you wake up to this simple and easy mindfulness practice, setting the intention for your day ahead to begin with a new outlook of peace and balance.

Instead of picking up your phone as soon as you wake up—and we are all guilty of doing this—stop scrolling and take a few minutes to draw your attention to your breath. As you lie or sit up in bed, close your eyes and focus your attention and awareness on your breath in your body. Feel the breath moving upward in your body on the inhale and feel the breath moving downward in your body on the exhale. While doing that, repeat the intention for this chapter to yourself three times, first aloud, then at a whisper, and finally silently: "I let go of excuses." Remember this intention throughout your day. It will serve as a great reminder to be more present and mindfully aware.

Intention 3
I am not my thoughts

In this chapter, we will explore the power of your thoughts to shape your reality. We will also outline accessible ways in which you can start bidding farewell to your negative thoughts once and for all. It has taken me years to slow down my mind and start feeling like I am more in control of my thoughts and habitual negative thought patterns. I remember a time years ago in London when I was having a facial and the aesthetician told me that she was going to leave me for twenty minutes while my face mask was on. I remember a feeling of complete panic and terror washing over me in that moment. Being on the bed, alone in a dark room that I could not leave, with no distractions but just my thoughts. My intention was to book myself for a facial to relax, not be tortured by my ongoing negative internal narrative at the time!

This was also coming at a time in my life when inner peace seemed completely out of my grasp. In my early twenties, life was about having fun and less about logic and reason or making decisions that served my highest good. I also tended to spend a lot of my free time being "busy" for no good reason and alone time became promptly filled with countless social activities that usually involved drinking, late nights, and the opposite of inner peace. When we don't make decisions that serve our highest good, we don't feel peaceful and you are not going to feel inner peace up in the club in my experience anyway.

Now that I am older and wiser and yes this wisdom came with a lot of kicking and screaming, when I feel a negative thought arise I am aware of it. This awareness enables me to negate the thought, or replace it with a positive one. Of course this is still a work in progress and some days are easier than others! I used to have a tendency to be the person with the ongoing narration in my head that was filled with judgment primarily of others and myself. I was also the harshest critic of myself, and it is interesting how these patterns of thought manifest themselves in daily life like an old, familiar but definitely unwanted friend!

Letting Go of the Inner Critic

I came to realize through the practices of meditation and mindfulness that the inner judge and harsh critic of others and myself served no place in my mind or life any longer. My new path of self-love and self-awareness started to replace the harsh inner critic. Old habits die hard, though, and I am vigilant as it doesn't take much for a negative thought to pop up and then the judgment kicks in leading you down the endless rabbit hole.

You can successfully begin to start changing your internal negative narrative by offering yourself three things that are an integral part of a daily mindfulness practice:

1. Self-love
2. Compassion
3. Nonjudgment

Through these mindfulness practices, I have effectively learned to slow down my mind and adopt a more serene and nonjudgmental outlook. This new attitude is filled with greater love and compassion toward myself and others through the ups and downs of my daily life. These are very useful tools to navigate ways in which to stop the constant cascading thoughts, often negative ones, from arising.

There have been times in our lives when we could be in the most idyllic place, that beach in the Bahamas or watching that sunset in Hawaii. Yet regardless of our amazing location we cannot escape from ourselves and our thoughts. It really doesn't matter *where* we are if we are chained to living in the prison of our own minds, with or without the exotic Instagram-worthy backdrop!

We have more than sixty-thousand thoughts every day, no wonder we feel anxious and like we live captive in the prison of our own minds! Our thoughts are repetitive and often negative, which feeds that background of anxiety and sense of constantly being ill at ease. If you feel that you will never be able to change your way of thinking no matter how hard you try, you are not alone. Many of us feel that we will never be able to change our mindset or successfully impact lasting change in our lives. It is very easy to become trapped in the cycle of constantly replaying the past or worrying incessantly about the future.

The past has occurred and the fact is that even what happened five minutes ago is unchangeable. Therefore, we must learn ways to accept our past and fully embrace our journey, both the negative and positive experiences that have gotten us to where we are today. When I reflect upon my own past, there is not much I would change, there are some things I definitely cringe at but it was all part of the journey. Meditation and mindfulness help us to look at ourselves through the lens of love, compassion, and nonjudgment and embrace ourselves wholly on our journey through life.

Look Past Fear-Based Thoughts

Our inner critic and fear-based thinking can keep us stuck. Meditation can help us move past those blocks to find our strength and purpose. We all have a strong mind-body connection, and I realized in 2015, after being rushed to hospital for emergency surgery after suffering acute appendicitis, that I was poisoning myself with my own toxic thoughts. This was largely due to my inner unhappiness with my work situation.

My job on the surface was great, earning a six-figure salary and being in a leadership position for a software company that afforded me the opportunity to travel and live a comfortable life. However, this career path was not my passion, nor what I wanted to do. Each day drove me deeper into self-doubt and misery as I questioned what my true purpose was and how I was going to be able to fulfill this underlying yearning for more in my life.

After my stay in hospital I had to undergo six weeks of physical therapy for a complication in my arm with the IV; another sign from the universe that something had to change! During these physical therapy sessions, I started to ask myself deeply what was important in my life and what I wanted from life. I had just completed my 200-hour Yoga Teacher Training at the Soul of Yoga in Encinitas prior to all of this, which I had done part time while working full time. This had been the beginning of questioning my true path in life versus the path that I was on with my current job. I had great fear of letting go of what I knew in the form of a secure job and regular paycheck to forge a new and unknown path ahead and I am sure many of us can relate to that feeling!

All of my inner insecurities and self-doubts constantly played in my mind as to how someone like me could be successful in running their own wellness business; a path I knew very little about apart from my own life-long personal practice and study of yoga, meditation, and mindfulness. That was when I had a breakthrough moment after a meditation session and realized that my own background, experiences, and trainings I had already completed were more than enough to set me up for the journey ahead. In fact I came to the realization that I had everything I needed within in order to forge this new path ahead. How many of us don't even consider the skills we *already* have to start making our dreams into something more than just fantasies?

It took a lot of hard work to manifest my dreams into a reality. I ran my business for almost one and a half years in my spare time before I was financially in a situation to be able to leave my corporate job and pursue my passion full time, I would meet my clients after work and run the retreats over weekends. I knew this would not be forever, but it was part of what I needed to do in order to build the foundation of a business that I aspired to be able to run as my full-time job. My meditation and mindfulness practice were my anchor during this time and paid off, as eventually I was able to pursue my passion as a successful full-time business.

Focus On Your Strengths

Before taking the leap of faith to pursue my business full time, I asked myself what else I had to offer to help me on this journey? I realized I had my Hindu background as a foundation and many years of formal and informal study of yoga and meditation spanning a lifetime. I had studied under different lineages and schools in the United Kingdom, Australia, New Zealand, India, and the United States as a foundation to build upon.

This is a good lesson to look at what skills and qualifications you do have in order to find your purpose and make your dreams a reality and work toward getting what you need in your spare time. This may be enrolling in additional courses, finding an internship or a suitable mentor, or volunteering. Whatever the case may be, nothing comes without hard work and dedicated effort. If you are unhappy with where you are at in life, nothing will change if you don't make a commitment to yourself and do something about it!

This is most people's stumbling block. Often, people complain about being unhappy in their lives but the inner critic and fear-based thinking holds them captive from changing anything, However, negativity takes up more energy in the mind and body than having a positive outlook. We'll look more at how you can shift negative programming to change the script in chapter 9.

Negativity Causes Stress

A negative attitude and feelings of helplessness can create chronic stress in the body, which affects the body's hormone balance and depletes the brain's chemicals required for happiness, resulting in longer-term, damaging effects on the immune system. We may think those posts on social media about positive vibes and letting go of negativity are annoying but they are far more true than people give them credit for. The next time you see one, read more about it as you may be pleasantly surprised by the impact adopting a more positive outlook can have on your mind and life.

I decided to let go of all of that negative internal chatter and instead began to visualize what life would be like running my own wellness business. This was an area that had brought me so much inner transformation and deeper meaning, and it would be so wonderful to spread this message and share this joy with others. My friends and colleagues had always told me that I was like a positivity coach, always there to advise and offer solutions, and many had told me to pursue this as a career though I scoffed at the idea at the time.

At this point in March 2015, I had a deeper inner revelation that the universe had been trying to get me to see for a while but I was too steeped in my own old thought patterns and negativity in my current job to notice. Therefore, the rug was swept from under my feet and I ended up in hospital and physical therapy as my wake-up call. Message received, universe—I hear you loud and clear! As a result I made the difficult decision to leave my job and walk away from everything that made me comfortable. The universe works in mysterious ways and sometimes we are made to get really uncomfortable in order to have the courage to make the dramatic changes we need to in our lives.

In May 2015, I left my safe and comfortable corporate job to take a chance on myself and pursue my dreams. I could not have made this decision without the support and encouragement from my husband, who has always believed in me, even when I doubted myself. Part of a negative inner script can come from those we surround ourselves with. Be grateful for the relationships in your life that enable you to be your best self. These are the relationships that we want to foster and spend time on nurturing in our lives. Too often we waste time on people undeserving of our love and attention and allow them to take up so much of our time and energy.

The lesson and moral of the story here is don't waste time on people who don't appreciate and value your presence in their lives. If I could only have realized this truth in my twenties, it would have saved me a lot of time and misery. This is something I talk about a lot with my patients and clients. Who we choose to surround ourselves with is a big part of this process of finding inner peace and letting go of that internal negative narrative. Sometimes other people's negativity can have more of an impact on us than we realize. Don't allow other people to dim your light, and be mindful of whom you choose to surround yourself with.

Feel the Fear

My first month of business without the comfort of my old salary was June 2015, and I earned a grand total of $100 for the entire month and found myself slipping into complete panic mode. I could not help thinking I had earned more in a month at my part-time job in retail at university when I was eighteen! All of my old demons reared their heads and I began to seriously question the decision I had made and how I was going to make my business a success. I spent some time in deep meditation and understood that panic and anxiety were the exact opposite vibrations that were going to bring success to my business and myself.

I did not have the luxury of fancy connections as a safety net or a list of big clients waiting in the wings to swoop in and engage my services. I also did not have the budget to employ a PR firm or publicist, and knew I was standing on my own two feet now. I was fully aware that I was going to have to dig deep to make my venture a success and be as creative as possible with trying to generate new opportunities and business. As a result, I made a decision to give my new venture six months and not focus on anything apart from each day, one moment at a time, letting go of all of my negative thoughts as best I could.

If things were not showing any progress within that timeframe, I would have to reassess and explore new options—like everybody else, I had bills to pay. But until my deadline was up, I vowed to channel this energy into giving my business one hundred percent of my attention and focus for the next six months, without thinking about the past or worrying about the future and feeding any further internal negative narrative. This was not easy for a type-A control freak personality like myself. Going with the flow is something I have had to learn through my meditation practice, and it did not come easy!

Don't Be Afraid of the Tests

This period deeply tested my faith in myself and my decision to pursue my dream, and it generated fears and worries about how this was all going to work out. I remember the anxiety that I felt as I was constantly projecting negatively into the future or thinking about the past. My meditation and mindfulness practices saved me from giving up, and instead enabled me to go deeper within myself to find the courage, strength, and self-belief to continue on my path.

I set myself a deadline of six months to see if I could make a success of it and vowed not to worry about anything—especially finances—until that six months was up. During this period, I stuck to a tight budget I had set myself and gave one hundred percent of my mindful attention, dedication, and commitment to my business. It is very easy to get dragged into the cycle of truly believing that we need more than we do and get into the mode of working to provide for more than we need.

We can become so caught up in the rat race of consuming, buying, and constantly upgrading that we lose sight of why we are actually here. Today's society is so consumer-driven that it is easy to get caught up in wanting more and more, with insatiable desires that will never be met. It's also easy to work just to fulfill these desires and constant wants rather than enjoy our lives as they are and cherishing the relationships we are blessed with in our lives. We must nstead spend more time and energy on meditation and mindfulness practices that leave us feeling much more fulfilled.

As I left the corporate job that made me miserable, I wanted to always remember and bring my awareness back to the fact that I have enough in my life just as it is. I wanted to value the things that can't be bought that I am so grateful for and to have complete faith in God and the universe that all of my needs will always be provided for. To not be afraid and get caught up in the steady income stream and spend my life not doing what my soul was screaming at me to do.

Having the courage to fully embrace my inner voice was vital in overcoming the fear of losing material possessions and my safety net and being strapped for cash. To instead have faith and trust in myself to create success in doing what I love. To also live a simple life enjoying the richness that life has to offer in family, friends, and the beauty of nature that surrounds us.

I have to say it is a great lesson in life when you go back to the basics and you cut out all of the frivolous things we spend our money on. It is good to know that you don't need any of the things you buy apart from the necessities of basic food and clothing. When we have money to burn we often buy things for the sake of it. Did you really need that eleventh crystal, ninth houseplant, or twentieth pair of shoes? There is nothing wrong with buying any of these things and enjoying them, I know I do! However, it is also a good lesson to learn to be unattached to all of these things and know that you don't need them to survive or live a happy and fulfilled life.

Finding Balance

Going through this process taught me the most valuable lesson: to trust and surrender to life without resistance, and to have faith in myself on my path of dharma in this life, which in Sanskrit and yoga philosophy translates to one's path of duty and right conduct. I had to put faith in the knowledge that appropriate opportunities would come as long as I remained calm and focused on my goals and my personal wider goal, of helping people through these ancient practices to find and maintain inner peace. In order to fulfill our true destiny in this life, we must make that soul connection within and open ourselves up to living from a higher state of being. This is when we are able to connect to the power of the universe and things really start to flow.

The vibration and thoughts we put out are just as important as the effort we put in. Our thoughts will either reap rewards or end up attracting the opposite to what you seek, as often can be the case in our lives. Where our energy flows our intention goes and this is a subtle but very important factor to be aware of. If you are constantly focused on what you don't want in life, that is what you tend to attract. Instead, try shifting your focus to what you do want and you just may be surprised what starts coming your way, especially when you are connecting to source or spirit from a place of authenticity and true soul calling without an attachment to specific outcomes led by the ego and that false sense of self.

Part of the process of learning to calm our minds is accepting the duality of life and that there will be good times and there will be bad times. Eastern philosophy covers this concept, teaching that suffering is an inevitable part of life and one which we cannot escape. There will be gains and losses along the way, and accepting this truth without becoming stuck in a rut during the bad times or becoming overly elated during the good times is key to finding balance in our lives and minds. Otherwise, we could feel as though we are on a roller coaster with constant highs and lows that can become very draining and taxing on us physically, mentally, and emotionally.

We all no doubt have been on or are still on that roller coaster of emotions, and it certainly is not a fun ride after a while! I remember when I spent years focused on the thrill of the chase thinking that this feeling of nervousness and excitement was a good thing. Note to self now that I am older and wiser, people disappearing and not returning your calls or messages is in fact not fun or exciting. Staying in toxic relationships drains you physically, mentally, and emotionally.

It may appear fun with the constant exhilaration of highs and lows but after a while you begin to crave that sense of stability and balance in your life. We all get that feeling when there are people or situations we should stay away from and your internal voice is screaming at you to not go any farther down the rabbit hole. Yet often we can find ourselves drawn to the very things that we know deep down will not bring us anything good.

This ends up wreaking havoc on our sense of self-worth, which can take a long time to repair and rebuild. Your greatest responsibility is to love yourself and know that you are enough. You don't need to be accepted by others if you are able to embrace and accept yourself. This is real self-love and there is strength and beauty in this powerful truth.

Happiness Lies Within

If we reflect, we can see that it is often through our most difficult and trying times in life that we are able to embody our spirit and find the strength we need from within. This is what gets us through those darker times, knowing that there is a divine or universal presence in our lives guiding us forward and taking us toward the light. The difficulty is remembering to look up to see the light, however faint it may be, when we feel as though we are unable to control our continual negative thoughts. In these instances, the light can feel very distant and sometimes we may feel that we are surrounded by complete darkness and that we cannot see the light at all.

The point we have to come back to is that if we are constantly looking outside of ourselves for happiness, we will never find it. This is a hard truth we need to stop and come to terms with. If we don't, we can spend our lives going from relationship to relationship and clinging to friends and family to give us the happiness we desire. We can search for this happiness in our relationships, careers, and material possessions or with travel and experiences. I have done all of the above over the years and I can tell you from my own learning that all of these things can certainly contribute to our sense of self and offer us temporary happiness, but it does not last. True happiness and peace must come from within, regardless of our external circumstances and situations.

Even if we have all of these things, a fulfilling relationship, great job, and financial abundance, we still so often see that people are unhappy and dissatisfied in their lives. I witness this so often in the lives of my clients and patients who on the surface have it all but are lacking the most important thing, which is a calm and peaceful mind. This serenity within leads to a sense of self-worth and true self-love—not that gimmicky version of self-love that social media and our consumer culture sells us but a true sense of compassion, love, and nonjudgment coming authentically from within.

Part of really developing that sense of self-worth and self-love from within is spending time in self-care practices and understanding that listening to your own needs is just as important as listening to and trying to accommodate other people's needs and wants. Many of us feel as though we need to do it all and be all things to all people, running ourselves ragged in the process. We constantly make excuses for why we don't make more time to do the things that we really want to in life putting everybody else's needs and wants above our own.

Comparison Is the Death of Happiness

Meditation and mindfulness practices teach us that we don't have to be perfect, and striving for perfection can be the enemy of self-acceptance and self-love. Another key aspect of this journey toward self-love and self-acceptance—and this is a BIG one for most of us—is learning to not compare ourselves to others. If we are all honest, we do it more than we realize. We all have a unique path to follow in this life, sometimes our path may seem unclear or what we want is not manifesting in our life the way we wish it to. Often, it may seem that what you want everybody around you has and it is very important in these moments to remind yourself not to compare yourself to others.

So let's keep it real and understand that life takes hard work, dedication, and commitment and comparing yourself and your life to glossy Instagram feeds or magazine covers is never the way to inner peace. Nobody's life is perfect irrespective of what they may be advertising it as. Meditation and mindfulness practices really help with letting go of worrying about what other people around you are doing and instead spending that valuable energy on focusing on what you are doing. Happiness has to begin authentically in our own hearts and minds first. Often we may say the right thing but our thoughts do not match up with our words or actions.

Whenever I catch myself about to compare myself to others or worry about what anybody else is saying or doing, I promptly bring my focus back to myself. You can do this by focusing on your breath and taking a slow inhale and a slow exhale to steady your mind and anchor it in the present moment away from judgment and comparison. Bring yourself back to your breath and what you can control—yourself. This is truly the best medicine for living a happier and more fulfilled life. Your breath is your greatest tool in anchoring you in the present moment and empowering you to really notice what is going on internally.

Your path is different from anybody else's and charting your own course in life is the greatest journey of all. We do not know what is around the corner and if everything that we want we will get. I look back on my own life at some of the things that I really wanted at the time that did not manifest the way I wished them to, and they turned out to be some of my biggest blessings. My life would have been quite different if I'd gotten what I wished for, but thank goodness things turned out the way they did. I am sure many of you are vigorously nodding your heads in agreement, thinking about your own lives.

Sometimes it is easier to compare ourselves to others than it is to actually take the time to do the work that we need to in order to effect change in our lives. The tendency to compare can also stem from fear of change, which is a natural emotion and one that is often the reason people stay in dead-end relationships or don't take the risks they need to in order to make a change in their lives.

We can get stuck in a rut doing the same things and expecting a different outcome. Isn't that the definition of "insanity," after all? What has helped me most in this area is to start instead to be led from within and focus on looking for validation from myself versus others. Our exercise for this chapter focuses on learning to let go of your internal negative chatter by giving yourself the validation and love that you are so eagerly desiring. It is only when we can start to give ourselves this love and acceptance from within that we can start spreading this authentically to others.

Exercise

Five-Minute Journaling Practice

You will need a journal for this exercise. You can start creating more inner peace by validating your own needs and wants and giving yourself the love and acceptance you so eagerly desire. Make a list of areas in your life where you are feeling unworthy or lacking. Once you have completed your list, spend five minutes in silence, drawing your attention to your breath and focusing on inner contemplation of what has come up from this practice. Then start to address how you can change these things by journaling how you can transform your actions, thoughts, and words around these issues. Now journal some areas in your life where you can offer more love, acceptance, and nonjudgment to others. This is a way for you to take your practice of mindfulness into your life to serve others.

Once you start to be led from within, which this list will help you navigate, you can begin feeling more self-love and peace. Enable yourself to let go of your internal negative narrative, and stop the constant comparisons to others or the excuses for why your life has not gone the way you wished it to. Start committing to making the changes you journaled in order to let go of the negative chatter and embrace more love and acceptance from within.

Intention 4
I embody courage and strength

In this chapter, we will deep dive into how you can overcome your fears by tapping into your courage and strength. We will break down how you can overcome limiting thoughts and beliefs through the practice of gratitude and the power of mantra. Fear is one of the most debilitating emotions and prevents you from doing what you know is most needed. It keeps you from going for what you really want in life, and a fear-based consciousness and the fear of change can have devastating effects on our minds and lives. The ego itself stems from fear—of not being good enough, of not having enough, of anything you can name.

So how can we let go of our limitations and fears to embrace courage and strength from within? Is it that from childhood you were always told you were not good enough, attractive enough, or intelligent enough?

Were you always compared to other people and made to feel that you were not good enough as you are? Did you begin to harbor self-limiting thoughts as a result of outside influence at a young, impressionable age into adulthood? You can't change the past, but you can change your present through the practice of meditation and mindfulness.

Mindfulness aids us in learning to embrace our flaws in a kind and compassionate manner. It allows us to own our own truths in a humble yet confident way and have the courage to be *ourselves,* which is more of what the world needs. All of us must be brave enough to be our truly authentic selves, not other people's versions of whom we should be or their expectations of what we should be doing. Ultimately, you are in charge of your own thoughts and vibration. Meditation helps you to have the courage to live fearlessly by tuning in to your own inner frequency and vibration.

Don't shroud your light in order to make others feel better or more comfortable. By all means raise, adjust, and cleanse it, but never lower it for someone else. The more we are able to step into our own truths and follow our real purpose in this life, the better off we will be. What we need in this world are higher vibrations and brighter lights shining around us to guide us forward so we can all shine brightly and be appreciated for who we are, thereby encouraging others to do the same.

The Power of Perseverance

Don't give up! Sometimes we give up just before a major breakthrough can occur in our lives because we get impatient or lose hope. When you are working on shifting your vibration, dig deep; it is going to take all the courage and confidence you have and then some. You will never see results if you don't put the effort in and then have the patience to wait it out. Remember, the last thing to grow on a fruit tree is the actual fruit.

Major shifts may not happen overnight but will happen with dedication and commitment to your goals. So believe in yourself, and believe that you can and most importantly do the work required to actualize your goals into a reality through the intentions and exercises outlined in this book and chapter. You will succeed or certainly be further along your path toward success than you were before.

We can spend so much time focusing on our goals for the future that we don't also take the time to look back at how far we have come. I know that for myself, especially at the outset of a new year when it's common to become overly ambitious about goal and intention setting that I can forget all the things I have manifested along my journey. Sometimes it is important to take a step back and celebrate where you are right now. Perhaps that is a good place, or perhaps there is still a lot more work to do to get where you want to be. Whatever the case may be, know that in this moment and in the coming year anything is possible.

Letting Go of Limiting Beliefs

You have gotten this far, so let go of any limiting self-beliefs that are holding you back and really go for what it is you want in life. If you don't believe in your own dreams, nobody else will. You have to fiercely hold on to your dreams even if others trample all over them. Often people crush other people's dreams, as they are too afraid to dream anything bigger for themselves. It is easier to criticize and poke holes in other people's bubbles than it is to turn that lens on yourself and do the work to your life for the better.

In yoga philosophy this is represented by the Sanskrit word *mudita*, which is a feeling of delight at the good work done by another. Through mudita, you are able to save yourself from much anguish by not showing anger, hatred, or jealousy for another who has reached their goal even if you are still trying to get there yourself. If only more of us could embrace this concept wholly in our lives, the world would be a different place!

What can help us along the path toward mudita is making a conscious decision to try accepting what is in your life without fighting, judging, or resenting it and just sitting with that feeling. Begin to feel all the emotions that may arise without attachment, simply as a silent and impartial observer of the mind. Rather than letting the past define the present, fully surrender to the now and embrace your journey in its entirety without shame or guilt.

Use this moment to fully awaken to the knowledge that the past has no power over the present and everything that you need truly lies within you. Once you fully accept and embrace your journey and yourself, the fear stops and you have nothing to be afraid of or run from any longer. In this moment, you become truly free to accept the notion of changing your mindset in order to change your life; within this lies true liberation.

When you learn to trust and surrender on your journey as the exercise at the end of this chapter will guide you to do, you can also accept the truth that what you want at the time may not be for your highest good. Instead, have faith that what is for you in this life will not pass you and learn to enjoy the journey along the way. When you start to tune in to your inner frequency, you can feel support and love nourishing you from within. Think of it as your soul radio guiding you through life and your breath being a key component of this as your anchor in life.

If you are able to find this peace from within, even if just for a second initially, this is what will keep you coming back to the practice. Learning to fully embody your spirit from within is certainly what has kept me coming back to my practice! The process of realizing that everything you need to calm the mind and find peace lies within you starts this change. This realization begins with creating moments of silence in between the sixty thousand or more thoughts that you have each day. The more you are able to create stillness in your mind, even if just for a second, the more you are able to work on increasing those moments. The result is a calmer mind and a more peaceful self.

Beginning a Gratitude Practice

A practice of gratitude can be so important to adopt in your daily life. Thinking of a few things large or small that you are grateful for each day can be a wonderful mood up lifter and help set the tone of your day from negative to positive. You can begin this practice by journaling at least one thing that you are grateful for each day. It can be as simple as being grateful for your morning coffee or time with a loved one, human or animal. If you tend to see the glass as half empty, good company may also help. It is proven that interacting with close friends or loved ones helps those of us with a more negative disposition. It is shown to bring a much-needed boost in mood and optimism, so remember that the next time you are in a slump.

Gratitude lists are an easy daily exercise to boost well-being. It is something that I really enjoy doing as it helps to elevate my mood instantly by drawing my attention to things I am grateful for. Being grateful is linked to more happiness, increased immunity, lower blood pressure, better mental health, and improved sleep. So get busy counting your blessings! With my gratitude journal, it also makes me chuckle going back through entries and seeing what I was grateful for back when I first started the practice. It also helps to remind me of how far I have come. If we are ready and open to accepting them, our lives change when we really open ourselves up to receiving love and the abundant gifts the universe has in store for us.

Being connected to your emotions is a very important aspect of a mindfulness practice because without building awareness of what is happening within you, you will never be able to effect lasting change. Journaling is a wonderful outlet for processing your emotions and increasing your self-awareness as well as a powerful act of self-care. The emotional release from journaling reduces stress, lowers anxiety, and helps us sleep better. We are able to let go of things that have been playing on our mind, thereby gaining control of our emotions and improving our mental health. Journaling helps us to become actively engaged with our internal dialogue and really start to notice what is going on within. We explored this in the last chapter and will explore this further in our exercise at the end of this chapter.

The Power of Mantra

The power of the universe is something that many people scoff at. However, it really is more about simple science; if we look at how amazing it is the way Earth rotates around the sun on its axis, following a defined path away from other planets' paths. Miraculously, the other planets in our solar system do this too. Such is the gravitational pull of the sun, which is not even a planet but a star that is billions of years old and ensures that life on Earth is sustained by its light and power. We take three hundred and sixty-five days to orbit the sun but many other planets take years to make their orbit. It is a wonder that we are not in constant awe of just how mighty and magnificent the universe is!

The universe really wants us to succeed in our lives. It is there to help us along our paths if we choose to believe in its limitless power and infinite miracles available to us in each moment. In Hinduism, the mantra and symbol *AUM* represents the infinite power of the universe as the sound of the divine and all creation. The letters A, U, and M are said to symbolize speech, or *vak* in Sanskrit, the mind or *manas*, and the breath or *prana*, our vital force.

The three letters are also said to symbolize the absence of desire, fear, and anger; when united, they represent the individual soul's union with the divine spirit. Many faiths describe a sound as signifying the beginning of creation, which is also what AUM symbolizes. I chant AUM daily in my mantra practice, and it is amazing how uplifting and vibration shifting simply chanting AUM or OM can be. This will be explained further in our final exercise for this chapter.

It is believed that Sanskrit, which is an ancient Indian language, was the mother of all languages and is also the language of vibration. Science teaches us that everything in the manifested universe has a vibration and when we are able to connect with this language of vibration, we are able to better feel and connect with the unmanifested. It is also said that Sanskrit has a very high energetic frequency attached to it, as the mantras are powerful vibrational fields of pure energy. When you chant a Sanskrit mantra, you can't help but feel its vibrational force and power (and, side note, yes, correct pronunciation is important when you chant Sanskrit mantras).

The Sanskrit root of *mantra* is *man*, to think, or *manas*, the mind and *tra,* a vehicle or instrument. In its entirety, a mantra transports the mind from a state of activity to stillness. Mantras protect those who recite and reflect upon their meaning. Mantras are vibrations; they hold a certain power when chanted with the right feeling, reverence, and pronunciation.

The effect of any mantra is most potent when we understand and absorb its meaning. There are so many benefits to correctly chanting OM. When we use the power of mantra, we enable the mind to be transported as the mind is focused on chanting the sound of OM and the body is then given a chance to rest and take in the higher frequency of this mantra. Chanting is shown to reduce stress and aid relaxation in the mind and body, which in turn helps the brain to function better.

Patanjali's *Yoga Sutra* says a mantra is something that keeps the mind steady and produces an uplifting effect on the mind and body. Its repetition is called *japa* or repetition yoga. So japa yoga is communion with Spirit and the universe. Many faiths have a japa yoga practice associated with them; in Catholicism it is the chanting of Hail Mary with the rosary, and in Judaism it is the Hebrew prayers that can be recited as mantras. In Islam are the ninety-nine names through which Allah is recognized and can be chanted using the *tasbih*, which has one hundred beads and is used to chant prayers. Reciting these various names as mantras is said to be a wonderful way to connect with God and rejuvenate from within. A mantra practice is universal and can be done anywhere at any time—wherever you are, your mantra is with you too. By repeating a mantra continuously, a part of the mind gets linked to that mantra. In this way, a part of your mind is tied to the divine or a higher cosmic force while the other part is engaged in worldly pursuits. Basically, you don't need to stay away from anything as long as you do not lose sight of this rope tying you to Spirit, keeping you anchored firmly in what we call in Eastern philosophy the duality of life.

Embracing Suffering

Suffering and happiness are a natural part of the human experience, and it is inevitable that you will experience both of these things many times throughout the course of your life. Most of us are quite happy to welcome happiness into our lives but tend to shy away from embracing anything that brings us pain, as we try to protect ourselves from suffering too much.

Why would we want to welcome pain into our lives? Seems like common sense that we would want to avoid anything that brings us sadness and grief. However, it is basically impossible to never experience negative emotions. The more we attempt to escape these emotions, the worse we feel. For this reason, many people choose to self-medicate through alcohol, drugs, food, bad relationship choices, and so on.

Another wonderful effective way to embrace our suffering is through a japa meditation practice. This enables us to bring our mind fully into the present and away from the past or future. It is why I have made a mantra practice a daily part of my meditation routine and one that I really enjoy doing. I use my japa mala or meditation beads that have one hundred and nine beads on them. The one hundred and ninth bead is the sumeru bead, which you start and end with so you know you have repeated your mantra one hundred and eight times. You can buy a mala or necklace and begin a mantra practice, which we will go into more detail in the final exercise for this chapter.

Significance of 108

The number one hundred and eight is very significant in Hindu numerology, as it is the divine study of numbers. It is thought to be related to the twelve zodiac houses and the nine planets in Vedic astrology that comprise the Sun, Moon, Mars, Mercury, Jupiter, Venus, Saturn, the ascending north lunar node, and the descending south lunar node.

One hundred and eight is very sacred in Hinduism as there are thought to be one hundred and eight sacred spiritual sights. These sights are dedicated to the goddess Shakti and called the *Shakti peethas*. There are also one hundred and eight Upanishads, which are sacred Hindu religious texts. In Ayurveda, the sister science of yoga focused on the body, one hundred and eight marma points are described and said to be the points of vital life force where two or more types of tissue converge.

In Ayurveda, the fingers are associated with different parts of the body used in a mantra practice. The top of the thumb is represented by the brain and pituitary gland and is connected with the planet Saturn, or Shani in Vedic astrology; it symbolizes discipline by filtering out our negative urges to drive us toward a higher consciousness.

The middle finger is related to our sinuses and is connected to the planet Mars, or Mangala in Vedic astrology, and represents vitality and our inner fire within. It is these two fingers that you will be instructed to use in a japa mala practice for this chapter's exercise. Through the exercises outlined in this chapter on mantra and a daily gratitude practice, you will be guided toward finding this elusive peace from within and maintaining it throughout your day and life to uplift your vibration and tap into your courage and strength from within.

Exercise
Five-Minute Mantra and Gratitude Practice

You will need a journal for this practice. You may also find using a string of mala beads helpful. When your fears start overtaking your mind, focus on one of my favorite mantra practices. Start by taking a few deep cleansing breathes through the nose and out through the mouth. Then take a deep inhale and on the exhale chant the sound AUM or OM, repeating this three times. If you have never chanted before, don't be afraid to try. You can use your mala beads for this exercise: with your right thumb and middle finger, move the beads in a clockwise direction, chanting OM with each bead. You can chant this 108 times until you come to the sumeru, the final bead. If you do not have mala beads, you can count using your fingers to help you keep track until you reach 108.

The second part of this exercise is beginning a journaling and gratitude practice. Journal at least one thing you are thankful for each day, large or small, ideally at the beginning of your day. This practice will enable you to set an intention for yourself and remind you of something positive as you move throughout the rest of your day to keep you grounded and grateful.

Intention 5
I live my life for me

In this chapter, we will explore how you can start dialing down all of the external noise surrounding you. We will do this by looking at the roots of meditation in the West and the practice of yogic concentration as a way to liberate ourselves from bondage within. We will also explore the importance of finding balance in our lives and the power of nature as a healing tool.

How many of us are constantly receiving unsolicited feedback about our life choices from family, friends, and colleagues? Add social media, television, magazines, and advertising to the mix and it began to dawn on me recently how much unsolicited feedback we receive every day. This feedback ranges from lifestyle choices to what we eat, where we live, who we date, where we travel, what we wear, and even our choice of hairstyle. If we allow ourselves, we become bombarded by this outside noise constantly, so much so that it begins to drown out our own inner wisdom. Throw in modern society, fast-paced lifestyles, and the onslaught of technology and it just gives you a headache trying to keep up with it all!

There is a beautiful parable about a frog aiming to reach the top of a tree. All the other frogs told the frog it was impossible, that she would never reach the top. The frog thought that all of the negative comments were in fact positive encouragement, urging her to fulfill her dream. She reached the top by turning a deaf ear to all of the negativity surrounding her. We can all resonate with the story of this frog, and I encourage you to take the lesson into your own lives.

Your perception ultimately becomes your reality. In the above story, the frog refused to engage in any of the negative chatter around her. Instead, she turned it into something positive and focused solely on her goal of reaching the top of the tree. The frog achieved her goal with perseverance, dedication, and unwavering commitment. This is the exact recipe we all need if we are going to find our true purpose within. As we progress on our paths, there will always be people telling us we can't, that it will never happen, and similar. The amount of times I have heard that throughout my life I have lost count!

We may have overbearing family and friends who feel they are looking out for us by trying to steer our lives in a certain direction according to their belief systems, and they often have the best of intentions. Meditation and mindfulness practices aid us in drowning out the outside noise. Other people's opinions are just that—opinions. If we allow ourselves to be swayed by everybody who has an opinion about our lives and what we should be doing, we will never get anywhere. Nor will we be able to make any decisions that have a lasting impact, as we will have no conviction behind them.

Concentration Is Key

Transitioning into adulthood, we need to believe in the choices we are making more than anybody else's and tune in to our own wisdom to guide us in this decision-making process. In yoga philosophy this is called dharana, the sixth limb of the eight-limbed path detailed in Patanjali's *Yoga Sutra*. This limb is related to concentration, without which one cannot successfully meditate.

Dharana is single-pointed concentration and focus. Quite frankly, we should really just call it "concentrating" as opposed to meditating. Without mastering this step, we will never actually get to a state of deep meditation. Concentration or dharana is the ticket to a successful meditation practice and holds the key to being able to control the mind and negative thought patterns.

If you put in the time and effort with no external noise deterring you from your goal, the path of dharana or concentration will lead you to where you have set your intention on going. We are not using the full capacity of our brains or our minds. Imagine what we could achieve if we were able to harness more of our contemplative power within, to create both material and, more importantly, spiritual success and inner peace in our lives.

The Litmus Test

Inner peace can be something that we spend our lives chasing but may often seem just out of our reach. As a litmus test, ask yourself this simple question: are you happy? Take some time to reflect on what comes up and sit with this. If there are areas in your life where you are feeling unfulfilled, then make a plan for what you can do as guided in chapter 3. Remember that if you are feeling unsatisfied in some or all areas of your life, nothing will change unless you start making changes.

The first step toward happiness can simply be to take a breath, slow down, and really focus on what is going on internally. My favorite saying to my patients and clients is the wallpaper of our minds becomes the landscape of our lives. Start to notice your own internal dialogue as it has a major effect on your external situation. It may have more than you realize, in turn directly affecting your happiness and sense of self-worth.

When I was pregnant, it astounded me how much unsolicited advice I received from people about everything from giving birth to breastfeeding to childcare, such as how much time should be taken off work, and the list goes on. It exhausted me, especially as I was not seeking any advice from most of the people offering it. What worked best for them wouldn't necessarily work best for me or anyone else.

We all have to find our own way through the journey and do what feels right for us personally. Meditation allowed me to release any fears I had around all of this unsolicited advice and just tune in to doing what I thought was best for my baby and myself and find my sense of self-worth from within. The more we journey within, the more we can nurture our own self-worth and tune out all of the outside external noise.

Finding Balance

If you are not able to find balance within, it is easy to become swayed by people around you. If our external or, more importantly, internal narrative is negative, it can end up turning us toward the darkness within and away from the light. Most of us have received programming from the day we were born about what we should like, what we should believe in, and what we should dislike. This conditioning stems from our parents' and caregivers' belief systems, but may not, as we grow older (surprise surprise), coincide with our own belief systems.

The discrepancy between the two creates resistance and guilt as we strive to find our own meaning of life as opposed to somebody else's. As we grow into adulthood, the most important voice becomes our own, and of all of the people on this planet, you talk to yourself more than anyone else does. It is that internal narrative that becomes key so you have to make sure that *you* are saying the right things to yourself. Through the practices of meditation and mindfulness, you can reprogram any negative conditioning that doesn't resonate with you anymore or is no longer serving your highest good.

We can become so focused on what other people are telling us that we forget to be aware of what we are telling ourselves. Be very mindful of your internal dialogue, as these are some of the most important conversations you will ever have. The conversations you have with yourself are pivotal to the practices of self-awareness, self-care, and self-love; yes, a lot of "self" going on here!

The path of meditation and yoga helps us to start tuning in as the impartial observer of our minds, without judgment or criticism but simply tuning in to what is going on inside. As I said before and will keep saying throughout this book, the wallpaper of your mind becomes the landscape of your life. Choose your thoughts wisely and be aware of the internal canvas you are creating. This is what you can control.

Control What You Can

There is a lot in life beyond our control, and yet we spend so much time and energy trying to control people and situations, leading us nowhere. What you can control is yourself and your thought processes, so a good place to begin this work is focusing on your own mind. Trust me, this will keep you busy enough so much so that you won't have time to worry about what anybody else is doing! Now when I find myself worrying about what other people are doing or saying, I bring myself back to being concerned about my own words and actions, which is more than enough to keep me occupied and all that I am in control of anyway.

The other part that you have to be aware of is to not give up. We often self-sabotage or tire and give up just before a major breakthrough can occur. We don't get to see the magic that could have unfolded if we had more patience to wait it out a bit longer. You have to put in the dedicated time and effort doing that internal and external work and also be patient enough to not lose hope or give up in the process. A mindfulness and meditation practice really helps you to find the commitment to do the work. Have faith that the right results for you will come. It might not look exactly as you expected it to, but it will be exactly what is meant for you.

What is meant for you will not disappear if you give it your all and remain unattached to outcomes. If you put in the time and dedication without the external noise that deters you from your goal *and* with the use of dharana, that single-pointed concentration and unwavering focus, your path will surely lead you where you are meant to go. Being unattached to specific outcomes is also imperative. Do the work, put in the time and effort required to reach your goals, and then let go of your attachment to how you think things should go. Instead, open yourself up to being led by a higher power that knows what is best for you and is guiding you forward on your path.

Meditation in the West

How did meditation arrive in the United States? If we look at the modern history of yoga and meditation in the West, it was in the mid to late 1800s that India experienced a popular revival in the science and spirituality behind yoga that was also a form of resistance to British colonial rule. Swami Vivekananda was one of the key leaders in this revival aiming to bridge East and West with the 1896 publishing of his book *Raja Yoga*. He was a direct disciple of Shri Ramakrishna of the Vedanta Society and was the first person from India to bring the teachings of yoga to the West.

He was a very important figure, as without him the west would not have been introduced to meditation so early. Vedanta is one of the six Hindu orthodox schools of philosophy, along with Yoga. Swami Vivekananda attended the World's Parliament of Religions Conference in Chicago in 1893 and gave a presentation on yoga and Hindu reform. People loved him, making him a public figure overnight and the face of yoga in the West.

One of my favorite places to visit is the Ramakrishna Monastery in Trabuco Canyon, California, where I go to meditate and attend Sunday services and Wednesday scripture classes. It is very important that we uplift our vibration by spending time with people who have a higher vibration than ourselves in addition to spending time in places that are designed to enable us to seek God, source, or spirit from within if we are to really progress on our spiritual paths. There are some places or people in your life you spend time with and you automatically feel uplifted by them or the energy of those places that have a higher vibration; this is a vital part of being able to drown out the noise and focus on our own truth within.

The physical practice of Hatha Yoga was primarily designed to facilitate the real meaning of yoga; control over the mind. The *Yoga Sutra* does not focus on physical postures but concentrates much more on using the eight-limbed path of yoga as a means to self-realization and liberation for the soul, of which the asana or physical aspect of yoga is one part. Yoga and meditation is a science of the mind. Through continued effort with these practices, we are enabled to bring the mind under our control and open up to our innate power within.

Tapping Into Your Power

My favorite thing about mindfulness and meditation practices is that they enable you to start looking for validation from within, not from everybody else around you. It can be difficult to harness your power from within. Often you may feel pressurized to succumb to what other people want you to do versus what you want to do. This creates an inner restlessness that becomes the death of concentration. So often I hear my clients and patients tell me how they have lived their lives trying to please everybody around them and how it has led to much internal frustration and lack of happiness in their own lives.

I am fully aware that nobody else can make me happy. My family, friends, and career can contribute to my sense of happiness and well-being, but ultimately I will always be disappointed if I am constantly searching outside of myself for my sense of happiness and validation. This can be a difficult concept to embrace, as in the West we are taught from childhood that happiness can be found outside of ourselves in relationships, jobs, material possessions, vacations, and so on.

Having success in life isn't about some random stroke of luck that occurs or fate or talent necessarily. It is about believing something so wholeheartedly that there is no other possible outcome apart from what you are setting your intention to be. Athletes and Olympic gold medalists use this tool all of the time; if they think they will lose a game or a race, they will. The mind is the ultimate shaper of our reality. The repetition of affirmations or positive intentions can also help, so I strongly encourage you to actually start repeating the intentions at the beginning of each chapter to yourself as you read the chapters. Work on carrying these intentions from the pages of this book into your mind and life.

Detachment from Outcomes

Success with these practices is having the ability to remain detached from the results looking a certain way and being open to receiving the blessings that are meant for you. What holds most of us back in this area is ourselves—we lack the self-love and self-belief to actually consider that we could make our dreams a reality. Or we are vilified and branded as arrogant or egomaniacs if we actually do have this self-belief, especially as women and even more so as women of color.

You are damned if you do, and damned if you don't. It is a crippling frame of mind that makes us too afraid to hope for an amazing future in case we wind up being disappointed that it does not work out, or publicly shamed if we go for what we wanted in life only to fall flat on our face with the naysayers waiting in the wings ever ready to swoop in and say "I told you so." Well guess what—it is far better to actually try at something and fail repeatedly than never try at all.

Trying and failing still allows you to be one step closer to your dreams. If what you tried did not work, the second time around you can try something different. Not trying at all is never going to get you any nearer to happiness or inner peace. A very important point to also bear in mind is that the people who say "I told you so" when things don't work out are often the ones who never actually go for what they want in life, preferring instead to rain on everybody else's parade and be negative Nancies or negative Neds. Drowning out the external noise and everybody else's opinions is a big part of being able to feel more peace and joy from within as we learn through meditation and mindfulness practices to start tuning in to our own voice and truth.

Social Media Pressure

Take a break from scrolling! We often look for love and acceptance outside of ourselves and spend our lives chasing after something that we need to start looking for from within. Only we can give ourselves the love and acceptance that we so eagerly desire from those around us. We end up being so disappointed when our sense of self-worth is not recognized or validated by others in the way we want them to. Social media can really fuel this in a negative way, as we begin to tally up in our minds how many likes or comments our posts are getting.

Let's be honest: you would not be on social media if you weren't wanting people to engage or like your posts, unless you are the person who never posts but just stalks everybody else. However, getting two likes or two thousand likes is not where your self-confidence should be coming from; if it is, that is a very slippery slope. Granted, nobody is delighted with two likes, but true confidence must come from within; otherwise it will always be fleeting. So why are we waiting for others to make us feel worthy of our own love and acceptance?

The Musk Deer

There is an old Indian fable that Sri Swami Satchidananda recounts in the *Yoga Sutra*, the story of the musk deer. This is one of the most endangered and rare species on our planet. These animals are unaware of their own beauty and roam all of their lives not knowing the value that lies within them. Male musk deer produce one of the most expensive scents in the world known as *kasturi* in Ayurveda. In Ayurvedic medicine, kasturi was used as an anti-inflammatory, antioxidant, antibacterial, and anti-aging agent. The scent is produced within the deer's own body, on the underside of its stomach.

The musk deer is unaware of its ability to create the scent and is fascinated by it—it seems to permeate all of its surroundings. The musk deer spends its life searching for this scent, roaming for miles and miles in mad pursuit of finding this beautiful aroma. A musk deer can even unknowingly destroy his musk pod by rubbing against rough edges of the Himalayas, damaging the very thing it is hunting for. The musk deer dies without finding out that all along what he was searching for was within him. If he were able to realize this truth, it would have given him a lot more inner peace and satisfaction!

If we too can live our lives for ourselves and learn to search for the beauty within by becoming our own best friend and supporter in life versus constantly searching for this outside of ourselves, we will see our lives transform in miraculous ways. So often we look for validation outside of ourselves and spend our lives searching for it in relationships, our careers, material possessions, or experiences as we are sold this false concept that all of these things can help us feel peace within. They can certainly contribute to our sense of well-being and happiness but ultimately the real work begins with looking for it and finding it inside of ourselves by tapping in to our own power and truth within.

Lasting joy and peace can only come from within and not without a lot of soul digging and toiling. With hard work and effort comes the reward, and when we find this inner beauty and peace, we realize that nothing and no one can take this away from us. Tuning in to our eternal soul or *jivatma,* as we call it in Sanskrit and yoga philosophy, is the true source of our inner peace and light.

The Power of Nature

A great way to connect to that place of peace within is by spending time in nature. From four weeks old my son has accompanied me on my walks in nature and it is amazing to see how much he notices and hears. It always surprises me when I see people on their phones or blaring loud music on a walk in nature, illustrating that even in nature we find it difficult to not look for external distractions. I always encourage my patients and clients to be fully present when they are out in nature. It is always a part of their homework, whether they are on a walk, at the beach, in a park or in their back garden, to be fully present.

To listen to the sounds of nature, notice the trees and the leaves stirring in the breeze. Hear the sounds of the birds chirping and notice the color of the sky and the formation of the clouds. It is amazing what we miss out on because we are not present, aware of our surroundings, or taking the time to look up! So much of our time these days is spent looking down at our phones that we are having neck and back issues resulting in poor posture. Plus we miss seeing so many beautiful things. I make it a point every day to look up at the sky and notice the birds flying, the blue skies, and the cloud formations. At night I gaze at the stars and the moon, which is my favorite as I am slightly obsessed with the moon and have been since I was a small child.

Spending time in nature is proven to have a multitude of healing benefits as we will explore in the exercise for this chapter. I thoroughly enjoy immersing myself in nature and use that time as a way to reset and release, bringing my mind into the present moment and enjoying the beauty of my natural environment, wherever that may be. It really helps me to reflect, reset, and let go of any worries or tension I may be feeling. The effect nature has on the body and mind is proven. Time in nature helps our ability to focus, increases our happiness, lowers blood pressure, and improves our mental health. Nature is healing and allows the brain to reduce negative thought patterns. So what are you waiting for? Get out in nature today and start reaping the benefits!

Exercise

Five-Minute Nature Practice

Find a spot in nature, even in your backyard or a nearby park or green area. Begin by closing your eyes and taking a few deep calming inhales and slow relaxing exhales. Focus on emptying your mind of your thoughts, worries, and any anxieties in this moment. Allow yourself to bring your mind and body into a state of complete relaxation as you surrender yourself to nature and repeat the intention for this chapter ten times: "I live my life for me."

Release the intention and start to visualize what you would really like your life to be. Perhaps focus on one thing that you have really been yearning for and start to imagine what that would be like, whether it is a relationship, good health, a new career, or a big move. Whatever it may be, really start to breathe life into this picture on your blank canvas and imagine yourself at your destination, having achieved what you wished for.

If your mind starts drifting to the negative in your visualization, use your breath to keep you anchored in the present. Tune in to nature around you, opening yourself up to the notion that anything is possible; if you maintain a positive outlook and keep dreaming it, you can do it!

Intention 6
I trust my inner truth

In this chapter, we will follow on from the last chapter by examining how we can learn to trust our inner truth once we have drowned out all the external noise. We will navigate this by looking into how you can empower yourself by finding balance within and letting go of guilt and shame. This release is key for successfully tapping in to your intuition and trusting your wisdom from within.

My intuition never guides me down the wrong path; the only problem has been when I don't listen to it! The good news is that we all have this inner compass and wisdom, every single one of us. The difficult part is figuring out how to tune in to hearing it and then learning to trust it and be guided. I spent a long time drowning out that voice until I realized that it really *is* on my side. Part of our problem is that we don't believe in ourselves enough to trust our inner voice so we spend our lives second guessing ourselves and the decisions made along our path.

Your instincts will never lead you astray. The only problem is that a lot of the time we choose to ignore that little feeling inside or are unable to tune our internal frequency to even hear that voice guiding us from within. As they say, hindsight is a valuable thing. How many times have you thought to yourself, "I knew I should have listened to that inner voice or feeling?"

Tapping In to Your Inner Voice

The next logical question is, how are you able to tune in to your inner voice so you can really listen to it and trust what it is telling you? How do you even hear it amid the outside noise? Unfortunately, we can't just flip a switch and magically hear this inner voice and solve all of our problems. It takes time and is often not an easy process to develop in order to fully build awareness of what is going on within you.

The good news is that you can develop this awareness through the practices of meditation, mindfulness, and the exercise and intention setting for this chapter. It is fully worth it! Once you develop this skill, it will serve you day in and day out without fail and help you in making far better choices in your life. Who doesn't want to make better life choices, after all? Without the time spent on self-reflection and drowning out the noise around me to really hear my inner voice and purpose, I would honestly not be where I am today.

When we journey inward to hear the wisdom of our soul, it can often be a scary experience, as we really do not know what will unfold and what course life will start to go down. It also brings to the surface things we dislike in ourselves, or fears that we have buried deep within us that we would rather not confront. However, it is only through this path of self-study or *svadhyaya,* as we call it in Sanskrit and yoga philosophy, that we can finally let go of actions and behavior in our lives that no longer serve our highest good.

Personally, I am ever ready to let go of things that are holding me back, especially in my own mind as this is the place where our limitations, self-imposed or otherwise, are planted and take root. Once you establish your connection to your inner wisdom, you are then able to balance that fine line between tuning in to your inner voice while still respecting and valuing other people's input in your life and encouraging it in a positive way.

Empowering Yourself

When you throw in added external pressure from family and friends, trusting your intuition in life can become so confusing. I have witnessed people who were more than happy to allow others to lead them and make important decisions for them. Some may think this is a great thing, absolving yourself of your responsibility to lead your own life. However, not having your voice heard in even minor life choices can result in lasting blockages being created within you. It can also contribute to a loss of confidence and ability to speak your truth, or even having the ability to know your truth and trust your intuition from deep within.

A recipe for success is establishing boundaries with yourself as to what input you will tolerate from other people, as well as being very clear within yourself of your own personal boundaries. It may help to start journaling or making a list of what things make you feel good in your life and what things tend to have a disempowering effect. It can be liberating to have a journal for effect. This could be something you start doing at the end of your day as a way of releasing the day and processing your thoughts and emotions in a productive way.

Knowing your worth in life, not being afraid to ask for more, and setting boundaries with people if you feel it is warranted are key to this process. Very often we may feel uncomfortable speaking our truth or asking for more in our jobs and in our relationships. We may feel unworthy or that what we have is good enough and we should stay satisfied and not rock the boat. It takes courage to speak our personal truths and honor ourselves. Sometimes it may seem a very daunting task to start taking the necessary steps toward emboldening yourself to voice your emotions.

It is also very important to feel empowered enough to be able to say no to people and know that it is okay to do so. So often we are afraid of letting people down, especially if we ourselves are people pleasers, that we end up taking on too much and wearing ourselves down in the process. Just as important is becoming aware of stealing other people's time and energy along with your own valuable time and energy. What has been a truly liberating experience is being mindful of my own time and personal truth and not overextending myself or feeling guilty if I am unable to meet everybody's expectations. It is vital that we find that balance in life in order to feel happy and whole but also not resentful if other's or my own expectations are not met.

Letting Go of Expectations

It is easy to become bitter if partners, friends, or family are not meeting our desires and needs. I used to have the expectation that friends should be available when I needed them and justified this by telling myself that I was always available for *them*, so they should be for *me*. Don't you love your internal justifications? The things we end up reasoning about in our own minds and making excuses for is crazy!

In essence, I was giving but unconsciously expecting to receive in return for my time and effort; without realizing, I had a selfish attitude toward other's time. None of this helps you tune in to your inner voice; in fact, it just brings you further away from the process of learning to be led from within. In my own experience and with my clients, rarely do the results come if we are not vocal about our expectations and having our needs and wants met while also respecting the needs and wants of others.

You must have clarity within to be able to articulate what you need and expect from others and be open to feedback. This can be a big stumbling block for a lot of people and some may find it very difficult to overcome. If you feel you lack the confidence from within, spend some time tuning in to your inner truth, which the past exercises will aid you in doing through the practices of meditation and mindfulness. Start to listen to your messages from within, as they are there and waiting to be heard. Very often we spend our lives drowning out the voice from within, as we do not want to hear what it has to say due to our own fears and negative thought patterns.

There was a period in my own life when I spent most of my time drowning out my inner voice, as I was not ready to hear it. I spent a lot of time in constant restless activity, filling my time with endless activities and pursuits that served as a distraction from really tackling what I was resisting in my life. It is often easier to focus on other people's issues rather than your own, and believe me—I did this well! You can spend your life doing this, wasting precious time in trying to dissect other people's minds and actions. How many of us are guilty of whittling away hours attempting to understand the actions of others without ever really being able to find the answers we are looking for?

The path of yoga, meditation, and mindfulness helps us to make that shift and create more balance and peace in our lives. It empowers us to be unafraid to explore with love, compassion, and nonjudgment what is going on in our own minds and dealing with our internal blockages and negative thought patterns. This is all we have control over anyway, versus expending so much time and energy worrying about everybody else's problems and issues. Think of all the time you have spent chewing your friend's ear off about drama that you really didn't need to be engaged in, period.

Don't Feel Guilty

Know that to maintain your sense of peace within, you must have faith in yourself and your own abilities. Don't ever feel guilty or ashamed for doing what's best for you. Having this faith can take some reprogramming, as you learn to let go of other people's expectations of who or what you should be. If you really have this sense of self-worth and self-love, you won't waste time dissecting other people's issues and actions or worrying about what people might say about your life choices.

I invite you to have the courage and faith in yourself and to know your worth, as you are more than enough. If there is an area in your life that has been lacking, have that faith in yourself to not be afraid to ask for more in your career or relationships, as we so often are. Don't be afraid to follow your truth and dharma, regardless of the obstacles that may lie ahead. The moment you start valuing yourself and making choices in your life that reflect this sense of self-worth and love from within, the more you see your life go in the direction toward greater courage and self-respect.

An Example of Following Intuition

In April 2010, I came home to London from a trip to Los Angeles to visit family. On this trip, I had a revelation that the United States was where I was meant to be. I had a great life in London and no intention of moving anywhere. Plus I had no job or visa, so there was no way at that point of achieving this far-fetched dream. Yet upon arriving, I announced my sudden desire to move to the States with no job or visa to a dear friend who picked me up from the airport, who told me that of course I would do it, as I always did what I said I would do. These were very powerful words, as I myself was not quite sure that I could pull this off.

Later that same day, I announced my news to a few other close friends who were equally supportive and encouraging. None of them told me I was crazy or that it would never happen. High fives to them all for being such great, supportive friends; it has been one of my greatest blessings in life to have these ladies in my life. This gave me the immediate confidence to go full steam ahead.

Leaving no stone unturned, I exhausted every contact I knew who could help me with this dream while visualizing, meditating, and praying for this miracle to occur. At some points, it really did seem like a pipe dream. I distinctly remember being alone in my apartment one evening in May of that year and really questioning if this was the right path for me. As I looked up to the sky as I often like to do to make that connection with source, at that exact moment the clouds parted from the moon, which shone brightly as a sign to me directly from the universe to keep believing. My inner voice urged me to move forward regardless of the obstacles in my path.

When you think about how powerful the moon is, it makes complete sense that we are fascinated by it and that there are now countless new moon and full moon yoga and meditation events that people flock to. The moon has fascinated all cultures since time immemorial and in Vedic astrology, which is the traditional Hindu system of astrology, the moon is considered our closest planet, moving every body of water on Earth.

The gravitational pull of the moon is very strong and if you think that Earth is made up of seventy percent water and the human body is approximately sixty percent water, it makes sense that we are all moon obsessed! The moon in yoga philosophy and Vedic astrology is Lord Chandra, who is the presiding deity of the moon. Countless yoga poses are related to the moon, and the moon is also said to represent our minds or manas in Sanskrit.

Channeling this power of the moon by taking command of my mind and thoughts led to my dream becoming a reality. Within six months of putting my intention out to the universe to move to the States, I had quit my job, sold my apartment, and gotten a new job that sponsored me to move to Los Angeles, which I did, making the big leap in October 2010. It is outrageous what happens when you truly believe that anything is possible and, most importantly, surround yourself with people who support you in your crazy dreams and endeavors.

Uplift Your Vibration to Raise Your Intuition

My other point for this chapter is to really focus on uplifting your vibration in order to attract the right people into your life. So often we attract the wrong people and wonder why. The more I am able to focus on uplifting my own vibration, the more I see the right people enter my life and the wrong people exit. People have come into my life for a reason and a season, and that is okay. Some people are only meant to be a chapter in our books or even a page, not the whole story, and that is perfectly fine.

Part of tuning in to our inner wisdom is also realizing that the people we choose to surround ourselves with is a big part of the process. Sometimes other people's negativity can have more of an effect on you than you are aware of. Don't allow other people to dim your light! When I am really working on manifesting things in my life, I meditate, close myself off from other people's negative energy, and know that I don't have to share everything I am working on in my life with everyone. In fact, I often keep a lot of things to myself or just share with a small very close circle of family and friends I trust until those things come to fruition.

Be mindful of telling everybody your business and the company that you keep. The older I get, I realize how true and powerful this is. So be mindful of oversharing, keep your vibration high, and surround yourself with people who are also vibrating at a high frequency. Try not to allow those around you to bring you down or project their negativity and issues onto you. They are on their journey and you are on yours, so make sure you focus on just *your* journey. Calming our minds and inviting a sense of peace and serenity into our lives is a key component in embodying your spirit. Without this silence within, you will never be able to hear your own intuition that is always with you guiding you forward on your path.

I remember another instance of this from a number of years ago in London, in January 2002. I was looking for a new place to live and needed a place quickly as I had to move out of my old place. I thought renting a room would be the best, most cost-effective option and found a place in the same area that I had been living in before that was nice and clean with a spacious room. I would be sharing with one other girl who seemed pleasant when I met her and dropped off my deposit to secure the room.

As I left the new place and was walking back to my old place, my intuition was screaming at me not to take the place. I remember thinking I should call the lady immediately and tell her I was not able to move forward and then cancel the check I had written. But I brushed it all off, chalking it up to my own hesitations about living with someone I did not know which I had never done before. It turned out to be one of the worst living experiences I have ever had.

This negative experience taught me a valuable lesson that I have carried with me ever since: to send love and compassion to those still stuck in their own negative cycles and the importance of tuning in and listening to intuition, as it never leads us down the wrong path. Things would have turned out quite differently had I listened to my inner voice on this occasion! I would have spared myself and my amazing group of friends the bother of having to stay at that place with me or have me stay at their places instead.

Thinking about your own life, how many times have you ignored your inner voice only to regret it later? Our exercise in this chapter guides you toward learning to tune in to your intuition and trusting your own inner wisdom and knowledge. Your inner compass will never lead you astray if you really listen to what it is telling you, not just what you want to hear or interpret.

Exercise

Five-Minute Heart-Opening Practice

Start by bringing your attention to your heart space and taking a moment to get grounded in this area by focusing on your breath. Then visualize a lotus flower being planted deep within the heart space. The lotus flower is very symbolic in Eastern philosophy, as it represents the duality of life and how we can all be like the lotus flower that starts its journey in murky, muddy waters but rises above it to bloom to its full potential in life, repelling the water and dirt.

Feel that by your love you are nurturing this lotus within allowing it to bloom into its full glory. As you do so, repeat the intention for this chapter silently: "I trust my inner truth." Start to feel yourself tuning in to your lotus blooming within, allowing it to reveal its secrets to you. All knowledge is within you, so start trusting the process of allowing your spirit to guide you forward on your path.

Intention 7
I live in the here and now

In this chapter, we will delve into what mindfulness is and the effect of stress on our mind and body. We will also explore the power of your breath and how you can make mindfulness a simple and accessible part of your daily life. It seems that no matter where you go these days, you can't escape being confronted by the word "mindfulness." It is the new buzzword and seems to be *everywhere* in books, on the front cover of magazines, and being talked about on TV and the radio. As you can't seem to escape it, you may as well jump on the bandwagon and see what all the fuss is about!

So let me ask you, would it not be a wonderful thing to have a calm and serene mind through the ups and downs of our daily lives? Imagine having the ability to learn ways in which to stop the constant cascading thoughts, often negative ones, from arising. Do you sometimes feel that you will never be able to change your way of thinking no matter how hard you try? Well, you are not alone! I struggled for many years to slow my mind down and have more control over my thoughts and each day is still a journey toward mastering this.

Mindfulness and meditation practices have helped me so much in beginning the process of rewiring my brain to think in a different way; to truly opening my mind to the beauty in each present moment. It all sounds so cliché, I know, but now when I have a negative thought arise I literally cut it off midway in my mind and tell myself I really do not have the time for it. With a baby, a business, and a household to run, I really don't have the time to waste on negative thinking.

The practices of meditation and mindfulness enable us all to befriend ourselves on our journey through life, embracing the ups and downs so we can actually begin to fully enjoy the ride. I know that in my own life the more I talk to myself as if I were talking to a good friend and practice more kindness, compassion, and less judgment toward myself, the more I am able to be this way authentically with others. I am still keeping it real and holding myself accountable, but I'm only doing that through the lens of self-love and self-compassion, which is far better than the lens of judgment, criticism, and self-loathing! Let's be honest, it can often feel like we are living our lives with the judge on one shoulder, the critic on the other, and that constant state of worry in the middle. No wonder we feel like we are merely going through the motions of our day, barely being able to enjoy much of it as we are trying to keep those three negative chatterboxes at bay. Learning through mindfulness and meditation practices to let go of that inner judge, critic, and worrier has been a true game changer for me, beyond anything I could ever have imagined.

I notice how much easier it is when I am able to do this and actually enjoy wherever I am much more. This is also a vital aspect of the ability to welcome spending time alone and being in silence as opposed to running away from any chance to be alone with yourself and your thoughts. Many people find this very difficult to do, as they can't dial the noise down in their own minds. You can raise your hand if you are one of these people and, if we are honest, it is most of us.

Silence Is Golden

Our fear of being in silence is one of the reasons why the television is always playing in the background, there is music on constantly, or we are always on the phone. Of course there is nothing wrong with any of those things; I love a bit of TV and music myself! I was never a huge TV person but I love music and it was always playing in the background when I was home or on the go. I realized that it was actually really nice to be in silence, and a part of my mindfulness practice now is having the windows open and listening to the sounds of the birds when at home or enjoying being present wherever I am when I am out.

Now I only play music when driving, which makes it much more enjoyable as it is not just background noise but more purposeful listening as I immerse myself in each song while of course not getting too carried away with the tunes and paying attention to the road! Our TV is barely watched which makes paying the cable subscription even more annoying; but when we do watch TV it tends to be a nice activity for my husband and I to do together. Rather than just mindlessly watching television, it becomes more of an intentional act and an activity that you can share with your loved one.

How Can I Practice Mindfulness?

Very simply, you can practice mindfulness by bringing your mind to the present moment, which is right now.

Not living in the past, as we often tend to do, playing the same old tape over and over again in our minds. Nor is it projecting into the future and worrying about what is going to happen. Instead, the focus is on fully embracing the power of the present moment, which is all that we have. The ancient science of mindfulness and meditation practices has now been scientifically verified by modern scientists and been proven to work. Neuroscience in the past twenty years has proven the correlation between meditation and mindfulness practices as a way to regenerate our brains.

Bringing the power of yoga, meditation, and mindfulness practices to my patients and clients is something that gives me *so* much joy, and it is wonderful to see mainstream Western medicine embracing Eastern wisdom and ancient holistic practices. One of the most liberating things about adopting a daily mindfulness practice is that it allows you to stop living in the past. In addition, it teaches you to not worry incessantly about the future. We are all often guilty of doing both of these things, neither of which is any fun, I might add.

This does not mean that you do not learn from your mistakes made in the past, nor plan for the future. It simply means that you are not a prisoner of your mind, either living in the past or projecting, often negatively, into the future. If you can do this, you can start the process of freeing your mind to be in a place of nonjudgment, learning to absorb the beauty of each moment with love and compassion toward others and yourself. As I always like to say to my patients and clients, thank goodness what we worry about doesn't actually happen. Most of the time we are playing out worst-case scenarios in our minds that are the making of complete nightmares.

Mindfulness is an ancient Hindu and Buddhist practice and can focus on bringing your mind and attention fully into the present moment by using your breath. Our breath, which is our life force or prana as we call it in Sanskrit, enables us to bring body and mind together. This allows us to live in the present and not be chained to our pasts or victims of our future. Often we live in the prison of our own minds, replaying the tape of the past over and over again and worrying incessantly about the future. Through mindfulness we are able to fully embrace the beauty of the present moment and live in the now.

It is liberating to learn to become unchained from your past, letting go of your own limiting thought patterns and beliefs that have been holding you back from actually being happy. The good news is that right in this very moment you can make the choice to become fully aware of the now and feel how deeply freeing this can be. This is when the beauty of the present moment can really begin to unfold and the magic can start to happen in your mind and life!

Become Aware of this Moment

The mind of the average person is restless, even when making a concerted effort to concentrate. When you try to focus or still the mind, you may often have little success as the mind continues to drift in various directions. I remember years ago when I first began a dedicated meditation practice how I would sit in silence and be able to do it easily. What I found far more difficult to control was my wandering mind as it played my to-do list back, things I was worried about, or I found myself drifting off in aimless daydreams. It made me realize how much our minds tend to wander and how unsuccessful we are at controlling our thoughts and our minds.

What I have found to be very helpful over the years is to focus the mind and attention on one task at a time. Giving one hundred percent of your attention to whatever you are doing in each moment is not easy but can become much easier with dedicated time and effort.

My suggestion and what has worked in my own life is to devote your entire will power to accomplishing one thing at a time versus trying to do fifteen things without any real success as your attention and energy is so divided.

The Effect of Mindfulness on Stress

Modern science is now able to prove the benefits of these practices and the effect of the breath as a way of resetting our bodies and minds. When we take an inhalation and we force an exhalation we activate the parasympathetic nervous system (PNS) response in the body. The PNS is the aspect of the central nervous system (CNS) that calms the body and interfaces with the vagus nerve, the longest nerve in the body and part of the autonomic nervous system (ANS). The vagus nerve controls our heart, lungs, and digestive tract and promotes relaxation in the body, basically our rest and digest response.

Through our breath and via slow diaphragmatic breathing, we activate the vagus nerve, which balances the stress response in the body. We are then able to regulate our heart rate and blood pressure, thus entering a state of mental and physical calm and relaxation. When you are feeling stressed or anxious, taking a deep inhale and a long exhale enables you to slow your heart rate and blood pressure down and bring your mind back to the present moment. Think of it in the sense that you have your body and you have your mind and it is your breath that interlinks the two together.

Yoga and physical exercise in general create so many feel-good chemicals and hormones in our brain that are then released by the endocrine system into our body. When we feel relaxed and content, the brain releases "happy" chemicals or neurotransmitters that affect us in different ways. Dopamine is our feel-good hormone and is associated with our motivation and ability to concentrate. Serotonins act as a mood stabilizer and prevent anxiety and depression. Endorphins can block pain and oxytocin provide feelings of love and trust.

All of these hormones can be produced in the brain via yoga and meditation practices which is why we see that yoga is everywhere these days, very simply because it works. Neurotransmitters are our chemical messengers that relay information from one part of the body to another. Mindfulness and meditation practices are the way for you to keep this internal process calm and in check.

What happens when we cannot slow the mind down or focus on the things that we need to in our day? Research has shown that we spend almost half of our waking time thinking about something other than what we are doing, referred to as the wandering mind. It would be great if the wandering mind caused us more happiness and peace in our lives, but in fact it is quite the opposite: it is causing us to be miserable, anxious, and ill at ease. We are unable to relax even when we want to and enjoy the things that bring us happiness.

Even when on vacation at the most idyllic location or having some weekend downtime, you can still find it almost impossible to turn off that constant mind chatter taking you away from the present moment and where you are physically at. No matter what we do, we just can't seem to slow our minds down in the constant whirlwind of to-do lists and the pressures of daily life. If we can't find happiness in our daily lives, we will never be able to find that peace within.

So how does this lack of being able to be present affect you? When something stressful occurs or we perceive something stressful to be happening such as when we are worrying or ruminating about a problem, the amygdala sets off the alarm system in the brain signaling the major organs in the body to get ready to fight or flee. The sympathetic nervous system (SNS) kicks into action, and the pituitary gland signals the adrenals to start secreting the stress hormones adrenaline, epinephrine, and cortisol. This is useful if something stressful is actually happening, for example, if you are about to give a big presentation or run a marathon. Normally though, this is not the case. Instead, we are constantly activating the SNS and living in that continuous state of fight-or-flight mode, waiting for the next crisis to occur. Over time, this causes a lot of damage to the body as unreleased cortisol from stress and anxiety builds up in the blood. The result can cause illnesses such as high blood pressure, high cholesterol, heart disease, heart attacks, stroke, weight gain, lower immune function, depression, anxiety, lower life expectancy, and the list goes on.

How can we combat this buildup of cortisol in the body and find an effective way to release it? The answer is through mindfulness and meditation practices! Mindfulness and meditation practices can shrink the amygdala, the brain's reactionary fight or flight center. The good news is that you can practice mindfulness anywhere and anytime by simply bringing your awareness to your breath. Our breath, which is our life force, brings our body and mind together. This really enables you to live in the present and escape that constant internal negative narrative replaying the past or projecting negatively into the future.

Mindful Attention on Breath

In yoga philosophy, your breath is referred to as your *prana*. This is the Sanskrit term for life force or energy within. Our prana also represents the vibrational force of all of creation. Through your prana or breath, you are able to regulate the functioning of your body. For example, when somebody is having a panic or anxiety attack, what are they told to do? Breathe, because deep breathing regulates the stress response in the body and calms the central nervous system down. Everything in your body is held together through your breath. Controlling your breath through the inhalation and the exhalation is what a yoga, meditation, and mindfulness practice is all about and is the key to unlocking the wisdom and power of your soul within.

It is believed that wherever your mind goes, your breath follows. If you are able to bring your mind under control through meditation and mindfulness practices, you are able to bring your breath under your control also. This is what the true purpose of yoga and meditation is about as outlined in Patanjali's *Yoga Sutra*. First you learn to control the physical body through asana or the yoga postures, which is the third limb on the eight-limb path of yoga. Then you learn to control the movement of the breath through pranayama, or breathing exercises, which is the fourth limb.

The next step is beginning the process of learning how to withdraw the senses through pratyahara, the fifth limb, followed by the mind through dharana, concentration, the sixth limb, and dhyana, meditation, the seventh limb. The final result is samadhi, or union with God or universal consciousness in the eighth limb. This is the reason we come to our yoga mats or meditation cushions and is what keeps people coming back day in and day out. When you catch a glimpse of what your body and breath are capable of, you want more and more of that feeling of deep inner peace and sanctity within.

Rewiring Your Brain

We can become so caught up in our constant negative internal narrative. We can't even seem to fully embrace the good in our lives or when things go well as we are waiting for the other shoe to drop, living in constant anticipation of something bad to follow. This is no way to live and is the opposite of choosing to embrace living in the present mindfully and intentionally. So you might now be thinking, well, how can I be happy in the present moment? The good news is that it is actually possible to rewire your brain through mindfulness and meditation practices. So you can begin to feel in control of your thoughts and not just be living at the mercy of them.

How nice would it be to actually be in control of your thoughts and emotions for a change. What you have to remember is that the mind actually does what it thinks you want it to do. Its main goal is to save you from painful experiences and move you toward happier ones. Rather ironic, I know, that the mind ends up being our worst enemy most of the time versus our friend! The reason primarily is because we allow it to run wild with no restraint or restrictions in place whether you are consciously aware of it or not.

Science has confirmed that via the brain we are able to adjust the chemical balance in our bodies and minds to feel those positive vibes. The hippocampus is the part of the brain that is responsible for our happiness, emotions, and where our short- and long-term memories are stored. We are naturally wired through evolution to pay more attention to negative experiences versus positive ones, as a survival mechanism and we are all familiar with this no doubt! The amount of times we focus on that one person who says something negative to us versus the ten people who said something positive. Or we obsess about the few people in our life who are not supportive versus being truly grateful for the people who are consistently loving and encouraging.

One of the most liberating things about a mindfulness practice is that it enables you to free yourself from your constant over thinking. Please raise your hands, over-thinkers in the group. After years of being an over-thinker and over-analyzer, I can honestly say that this is truly the root of creating problems that don't exist. Committing to a regular meditation practice also allows you to focus on your thoughts, emotions, and actions in a way that is productive—so self-study versus self-flagellation. Most of us who spend time over-thinking and over-analyzing have a tendency to be far more critical of ourselves, berating ourselves for mistakes made which is hardly the path to inner happiness.

Neuroplasticity

The good news is that mindfulness and meditation can help rewire your brain to transform your life. Research has shown that through these practices you are able to create new neural circuitry in your brain, altering your brain and mind in order to change your life. The more you are able to detach from the thoughts that are not serving your highest good, the more you become mindful of the internal wallpaper of your mind. Then you will be better equipped to start replacing those negative thoughts with more positive ones.

The ability of the brain to vary or change its patterns is called neuroplasticity. In the last twenty years, neuroscience has proven the correlation between meditation and mindfulness practices as a way to regenerate our brains and minds. The bombshell is that you are able to control the way your mind works if you can control your thoughts. This all comes back to how important it is to be mindfully present with your thoughts so you can keep your internal narrative under control.

Creating Your Own Superpower

Mindfulness doesn't solve all of your problems and make them magically turn into puppies and rainbows. Nor is it an excuse to avoid exploring what is going on within such that you turn into an emotionless shell. Mindfulness is in fact the opposite of this and allows you to control your emotions more by having a heightened awareness when a negative emotion or thought arises and then be able to process it in a constructive manner. Think of mindfulness as your superpower and yourself as the new comic book heroine or hero with meditation and mindfulness as your armor. Can't wait for that comic book to come out! In yoga philosophy, it is said that mindfulness is a wonderful way to create dynamic willpower to form good habits.

The *Yoga Sutra* talks about how restraining the mental modifications of the mind is actually the practice of yoga and the reason we do it. If you are able to do this, then you have achieved the goal of yoga. It sounds easy but in practice is obviously far more difficult. The *Yoga Sutra* says that the entire outside world is based on our own thoughts, as our thoughts then become our reality. This is why the practice of yoga and meditation is not concerned with changing the external world but focuses on changing your internal landscape. How you view the world through the lens of your mind and thoughts in turn affects your experience with the world around you.

Mindfulness works. Like anything, though, you have to do it. The more you practice, the easier it becomes, and this is how over time it becomes your superpower. Our exercise for this chapter will aid you in the process of making a daily mindfulness practice an accessible and easy part of your life. Learn to let go of the past and live fully in the here and now. The present moment is the only place that we can really embrace and experience joy and peace from within.

Exercise

Five-Minute Chakra-Balancing Practice

Set your alarm for five minutes. Come to a comfortable seated position in a chair or on the floor; you can also do this practice lying down. Wherever you are, ensure the spine is in a neutral position, so remove any cushions or pillows from underneath your head or neck so the cervical spine can remain long. Gently close the eyes if that feels comfortable to you or you can remain with the eyes open. Begin by taking three deep audible inhales and exhales in through the nose and out through the mouth. Once you have completed the three rounds of that breath work pattern, release, returning to your normal rhythm and pattern of breathing.

Gently feel that you are relaxing all of the muscles in the head, neck, and shoulders. Release the tongue from the roof of the mouth and relax the point between the eyebrows. Slowly and gently allow your mind to settle in that place of stillness and quiet within, letting go of all of your daily cares and concerns. You have none of those things in this moment. All that you have is your breath. Now take your attention to the chest and belly area and become aware of the movement there as you breath. Notice how the breath feels in this space.

Now do a complete scan of your body, noticing if there is any tension residing in any other parts of your body. Use your breath to move to those parts of the body that may be feeling tight or tense. Breathe space into these areas of tightness, allowing the oxygen and blood to flow more freely through these spaces. After your body scan is complete, sit with your breath focusing on each inhale and exhale, silently repeating the intention: "I live in the here and now" until your alarm rings signaling the end of your practice.

Intention 8
I embrace my pain

In this chapter, we will uncover helpful ways to process our internal pain and suffering through greater acceptance, nonjudgment and self-compassion. The more we are enabled and empowered to love ourselves, the more we can focus on spreading this love to others authentically. If we are living in the prison of our own minds filled with judgment and negative thoughts about others, and ourselves, we will never be able to tame the tiger within us. This tiger feeds off all of our internal negative narrative. The path toward learning to control our inner dialogue is steeped in self-love and self-acceptance.

If we are unable to love ourselves fully and accept ourselves without judgment, we will continue to suffer and possibly project our wounds and pain onto those around us. Somehow, no matter how hard we try, we just can't seem to find the right methods to calm our inner tiger. We don't know what to do to stop it from wanting to react to everyone and everything that pushes our buttons. Once our buttons are pushed, our inner tiger will bite indeed! If we start to become aware that this path leads us nowhere and away from what we seek, we can then find inner peace.

Inner peace is a common desire among us all, no matter what part of the world we may be from. A very important lesson I have learned over the years is to detach from a lot of internal dialogue, especially the thoughts focused on judgment of others and myself that do not serve my highest good. Part of the journey of mindfulness is having compassion for ourselves with our own internal judgments and criticisms and we all have these negative thoughts. It is also important that we are open and honest with ourselves about our own biases and judgments as we all have them. It is only through awareness that change is possible.

It is unrealistic to believe that we will be happy and positive all of the time. The human experience is to feel sadness, anger, jealousy, envy, guilt, shame, and the other emotions opposite the positive ones, such as happiness, love, peace, contentment, and joy. The point of a mindfulness practice is not to force feelings of happiness or positivity all of the time, as that often makes us feel worse and is counterproductive as it does not deal with the root cause of why we are feeling these negative emotions in the first place. We must examine our own pain through the lens of love and compassion. It is our own inner pain and unhealed trauma that can end up making us so reactive.

You will never be able to heal these deep-rooted wounds if you don't start to explore your common triggers and reactors. Why do you always react in a certain way when someone pushes your buttons? If you explore your reaction at a deeper level, you may realize that how you react to one negative thing in your life is how you react to many things, whether they are related or not. So what is the solution to being able to calm your over-reactive tiger within?

The path of meditation and mindfulness is to learn to be an impartial observer of the mind, which is a pivotal part of the process of calming your inner tiger and telling it "easy tiger" versus being constantly on the defensive and in attack mode. Notice what arises. If negative thoughts are arising, which they will, allow yourself to work on getting to the root cause of why you are feeling that way. This is one of the most important tools in your mindfulness and meditation practice, as this is what can set you free.

You will begin to realize that you are not every single thought that you have, negative or positive. In particular, the negative ones tend to stick with us. The more we are able to tune in and see what is really going on in our minds, the better able we are to control our thoughts. Through awareness comes change. If we are not even aware of our own internal dialogue in each moment, than we will never be able to regain control of our minds and habitual negative thought patterns.

Positive Self-Communication

Communication is also key to success in life whether in relationships, with family or friends, or in the workplace. How we communicate enables us to manifest our truth in our lives. And the most important part of communication is self-communication, something a lot of us are not even aware of. People often lament the fact that they do not get the desired responses they want out of situations or from people in their lives, but it all comes back to how we communicate with ourselves. Of all of the people on this planet, you talk to yourself more than anyone else does. Make sure that you are saying the right things.

Begin to ask yourself: what is your internal dialogue? How do you react when things go wrong or when they go right? Are you dejected at the slightest form of rejection in your life or do you stand strong and tall in the face of adversity, which is a necessary part of life? When things are going well, are you overly elated and jubilant about life only to fall very hard when things take a sudden change of direction? Start to become aware of the landscape of your thinking and the thoughts that run through your head on a daily basis. It is through awareness that change is possible and often we are not even conscious of the constant dialogue going on within our own minds.

Sometimes we can be so focused on what other people are telling us that we forget to be aware of what *we* are telling ourselves! Be mindful of your own internal dialogue, as these are some of the most important conversations you will ever have. The path of yoga and meditation helps us start tuning in as the impartial observer of the mind. We call this in yoga philosophy and in Sanskrit the *sakshi,* or inner witness.

A key element of a meditation and mindfulness practice is learning to start observing our thoughts without attachment, judgment, or criticism by simply bringing awareness to what is going on inside. As I always like to say to my patients and clients, the wallpaper of your mind becomes the landscape of your life. So choose your thoughts wisely and be aware of the internal canvas you are creating.

The Journey of Self-Acceptance

Without self-love and self-acceptance, we will never allow the mind to enter a state of peace and balance. We will always be at the mercy of our fluctuating thoughts. We call this in yoga philosophy the ability to learn to control our mental modifications. In Patanjali's *Yoga Sutra*, this is called *yogas citta vrtti nirodhah*. In essence, if you are able to achieve this somewhat lofty goal, you have achieved the goal of yoga. I might add this is certainly easier said than done! However, with dedicated practice, it can be achieved.

The nature of the mind is to wander, which is why in Eastern philosophy we call this the monkey mind. Picture a monkey in the forest, jumping from tree to tree without much thought or care, wreaking havoc in the process. The mind has a similar restless nature that can become uncontrollable if left unchecked. It is why most of us are not living in the present moment, as we are not able to control our minds and thoughts enough to do so. It all sounds good when you read about mindfulness and opening yourself up to the beauty of the present moment, blah blah blah, but clearly this is much more difficult than it sounds, or we would be walking embodiments of inner peace all of the time.

So how do we get there or at least experience a whiff of this inner peace stuff? Learning to become unchained from your past is the first step in this process. Many of us allow our past experiences, good or bad, but let's be honest mostly bad, to define us. We punish ourselves for things that happened in the past and refuse to forgive ourselves, even if we were victims of other's harmful behavior.

The second part is learning to let go of your own limiting thought patterns and beliefs that have been holding you back from finding love and happiness within. Right in this very moment, you can become fully aware of the now and feel deeply how freeing that can be as you start the process of disengaging from that ongoing negative internal narrative. This is when the beauty of the present moment can really begin to unfold and the magic can start to happen in your mind and life. Yes, blue skies and sunny days await you through these practices!

Make a conscious decision today to try accepting what is in your life, without fighting, judging, or resenting it and just sit with that feeling. The concept of accepting what is in my life has helped me immensely to not waste precious time and energy wishing things to be other than what they are. Instead, I focus on accepting what is and the reality of my situation, which in turn aids me in conserving my vital energy and power toward manifesting my dreams into reality versus just complaining or pipe dreaming. It can also bring awareness within ourselves that many of our obstructions begin in our own minds and hearts.

Acceptance Versus Resistance

An example of when I was able to practice acceptance versus resistance was when I was twenty-four years old; I lost a kidney as a result of a botched operation to remove a benign tumor that was growing in that kidney. Through the practices of meditation and mindfulness, I was able to accept what was. I was able to let go of anger and frustration around what had happened. I could have spent years being bitter or angry about the fact that through someone's incompetence, I had lost a perfectly good kidney. Instead, I chose not to dwell on something that I could not do anything about or change the outcome of.

So often, we waste so much precious time and energy wishing things to be different than what they are. The more you are able to learn to accept what is in your life, the easier things become as you stop resisting the flow of life. I am not saying I was able to do this overnight and it was certainly a process! I had to put in the time and effort in enabling myself to let go of the fear and resentment that was holding me back from living in the present and accepting the situation as it was.

The medical team cautioned against doing anything that could risk bringing harm to my remaining kidney. When I told them that I wanted to learn to do martial arts, snowboard, and surf, they laughed and said that I was crazy and would have to be much more cautious now with my life choices. I allowed myself to feed that fear and for a year walked around like I was wrapped in cotton wool, not even going for a massage because I was so fearful of something happening in a deep tissue manipulation. After a year of living like that, I realized through my meditation practice that this was in fact no way to live. I vowed to myself that I would no longer continue to be burdened by my fear-based consciousness.

Instead, I chose to rewire my thoughts and have faith that everything would be fine. I went on to do all of the things that I wanted to but had been putting off because of fear. Fear, as I said before, is debilitating and robs us of our power. We get stuck in a negative rut thinking that we are much weaker than we really are. It becomes like venom to our inner peace and our belief in ourselves to overcome the obstacles faced in life.

Fear is also destructive to our health and physical and mental well-being. If left unchecked, those fear-based thoughts take root in your subconscious mind and germinate, filling your mind with poisonous fear plants bearing fear fruits. If you are thinking "enough already with the fear analogy," I am painting this morbid picture to ensure that you take this paragraph seriously and act upon it accordingly!

I took my fear around losing my kidney head-on and did all of the things I had wanted to try but was too afraid. I enrolled in a local Wing Chun martial arts program in London. I learned to snowboard in Bariloche, Argentina, and surfed my first waves, or should I say wave, as it took a lot of practice to actually stand up successfully in Itacaré, Brazil. I also enjoyed my first massage after the loss of my kidney in Granada, Spain, at the most amazing Moorish bath. I realized a massage was not going to make me self-destruct and have continued to enjoy them ever since. That of course does not mean I disregarded the medical advice they gave me. It simply means that after a long period of time, I refused to let myself be defined by narrow limitations when I knew I was perfectly physically capable of engaging in these activities.

Your Energy as Thoughts

Part of the process of rewiring my fear-based consciousness was to start observing my own thoughts and become more mindful of how this energy was affecting myself. It is impossible to be positive all the time, and life is about balance and embracing with love and compassion all of the emotions that we feel on a daily basis, good or bad. We are the result of our energy and this shapes our minds and in turn our lives.

I realized that I was solely in charge of my own energy and thoughts, and by refusing to give in to this internal negative narrative, I was able to change my perception of things and in turn my life. So if you can master this and accept what is in your life wholly and with awareness, you can begin the process of changing your internal dialogue from negative to positive.

Begin this process by feeling all of your emotions and thoughts that may arise without attachment to them, simply as a silent and impartial observer of the mind. Rather than letting the past define the present, fully surrender to the now and embrace your journey in its entirety without shame or guilt. Use this moment to fully awaken to the knowledge that the past has no power over the present and everything that you need truly lies within you.

Allow yourself the opportunity as you drown out all of the internal and external noise to begin the journey of going within to discover your light within and lasting inner peace. In this moment, embrace the feeling of changing your mindset from within in order to change your life. No matter what your circumstances or situation is in life, you can learn to let go and not be defined by the past or situations and people who have caused you pain and suffering.

Embracing Our Pain

If someone has hurt you recently or in the past, try to work on forgiveness toward that person. The best revenge is no revenge. The more we resist our current situation, the less able we are to embrace the lesson there for us—and there always is one! We can get so caught up in ongoing negative narratives in our heads. When we learn to forgive ourselves, we can work on forgiving people who have caused us pain in our lives. A meditation and mindfulness practice really enables you to work on letting go of things that are no longer serving you in body or mind. It also helps you to work on sending those people love and compassion, as they need it more than you may realize. To ultimately move on, let it go and be happy.

Life is too short to hold grudges or negative feelings toward people, as the only person that it ends up affecting is you and your vibration. One of the reasons I love the practice of yoga, meditation, and mindfulness so much is that it enables us to continue to evolve in every way. There is always room for personal growth and self-improvement, and there is always time to change our ways and habits to improve our lives. It is never too late to start living our best lives and be the best versions of ourselves we can be. If we work on changing little things about ourselves first and practice having more love, compassion, and nonjudgment in our hearts and minds, bigger changes will follow naturally.

Just because the process hurts does not mean the results won't be beautiful. Sometimes you have to go through the fire or *tapas,* as we call it in yoga philosophy, in Sanskrit translating as "to burn away impurities." Tapas is one of the niyamas that are part of Patanjali's eight-limbed path of yoga and are our personal observances. In order to advance on your path, you have to burn away the things that have been holding you back and create space for new things to come. You have to maintain the dedication and discipline required to rid your mind of poisonous thoughts and your life of toxic people. This will guarantee to uplift your vibration and your life.

If you continue to stay in negative situations, with negative people, your life will never be transformed for the better. You have to believe and work toward creating lasting positive change in your life. So don't give up on your way through the fire, as it is a necessary part of your evolution. Good things *will* come, and no work that you ever do on yourself is ever wasted. Keep the faith, as the most amazing things in life tend to happen right at the moment that you're about to throw in the towel and give up.

I think back to my own life when I felt that life was really testing me. Just as I was about to give up on a dream, something happened to show me that the universe had my back and was guiding me and protecting me on my journey forward. If something is meant for you and your highest good, it will happen. It may not happen exactly how you pictured it or in your time frame, but things unfold at the right time they are meant to. As I have said before, what is for you will not pass you so do the work, be patient and let things come to you. Our exercise in this chapter will guide you toward being able to let go of that internal negative chatter, learning to calm and control your mind and to tame that tiger within!

Exercise

Five-Minute Visualization Practice

Bring to mind some of your persistent negative thoughts. Now visualize a pair of scissors cutting these negative thoughts. Then either replace them with positive thoughts if you are able to or simply bring your attention back to your breath and the present moment. This is one of my favorite visualizations and one I use all the time. I have also seen my clients and patients have great success with this simple exercise.

It enables you to begin the process of training the mind away from habitual negative thought patterns and toward a more accepting and less judgmental way of thinking that serves your highest good. Do this as many times as you need to in your day. Do it fifty times if you need to! The more you do it, the easier it will become to stop those negative thoughts in their tracks.

This process will also really aid you in starting to tune in to becoming the silent observer of your mind and creating more awareness of the thought patterns you are having in your daily life. It is only through awareness that change is possible.

Intention 9
I love and accept myself

In this final chapter, we will focus on how you can love and accept yourself wholly and fully and reprogram your past pain and trauma into love and acceptance. We will also explore the power of sleep as a way to embrace more self-love and self-care in your daily life. Are you ready to let go of your negative thoughts and change that sad old tape that keeps constantly playing in your mind? Because this chapter is going to tell you how it can be done. That's right, every single one of us has the ability to let go of our negative thought patterns and embrace a new, more positive way of thinking. Most of our emotional responses to situations are learned behavior from our formative years and the development of our brains in the first few years of our lives.

Not all of our destructive thoughts come from traumatic events. It is the repetition of thoughts that stay with us becoming the landscape of our thinking patterns. Perhaps we tell ourselves constantly that we are not good at something or that we are not good enough or other people have consistently told us this in our lives. What can occur as a result is a learned pattern of behavior of self-defeat and fear that leaves us feeling powerless to battle our inner demons successfully.

Even if you unlearn a negative experience, it still leaves an impact on your mind that can lie dormant in your brain until you experience something that causes you fear again. Then your habitual negative thinking kicks into gear magnifying other emotions such as anger, fear, and frustration, which leads to guilt, shame, and sadness. You start to replay in your mind all of your past failures and setbacks like a sad tape on a loop. This tape doesn't focus on highlighting your current strengths but instead exaggerates future obstacles, leaving you feeling more powerless, depressed, and anxious than before.

Your Mind Is Trainable

Do not be disheartened, though, as there is light at the end of the tunnel. News flash: we can all train our minds and brains to be more open and receptive and less reactive and negative. Our brains have been scientifically proven to be highly trainable and malleable. We can do all of this through our breath, so the good news is you have what you need already in order to be successful. I recall from my own life a pivotal moment of inner demon battling when I went on a solo backpacking trip to Colombia in September of 2009.

It had always been a dream of mine to become a certified diver and I decided that I was going to make the commitment to doing this in the beautiful small fishing village of Taganga. I had a lovely diving instructor who was very kind and patient. I distinctly remember when it was time to complete my certification the two things I had been really worried about as part of the test were taking my diving regulator off and clearing my eye mask of water.

The day of the final exam arrived, and my diving instructor and I were at the bottom of the ocean. Thankfully, the removal of the diving regulator portion had gone smoothly. I was making good progress with all of the other tasks and my final task was to clear my eye mask of water that you purposely fill it with. As the water filled my eye mask, I started to panic as I just could not seem to clear it no matter what I did. I gave the signal to Victor that I was going to admit defeat and tried to start making my way back up. In that moment, my instructor held my shoulder gently and looked directly into my eyes signing to me in diving code that I could do this and to give it another try.

In that split moment I knew I had a choice. Instead of giving in, I decided to focus my mind completely on my breath and chose to let go of all of the negative chatter that was erupting in my mind. I brought my mind fully to the present through focusing on my inhale and exhale (and trust me when I say that nothing makes you more conscious of your breath than being under water and relying on an oxygen tank to breathe!).

I told myself in that moment that I could do it… and I did! After successfully completing the exam, we came up for air and my instructor gave me a hug, telling me that he knew I could do it, and I promptly burst into tears. It was one of those life epiphany moments where I realized I could do anything I put my mind to. I sobbed uncontrollably, freeing myself of so many of my old self-limiting negative thought patterns, feeling the ocean cleansing me of things that had been holding me back in my life inhibiting me from moving forward.

Releasing the Past

It's amazing what you don't realize you are holding on to. I like to explain this to my patients and clients in the following way. When you are born in this life your load is light, as you progress through life from childhood, to adolescence and then adulthood, you start putting all of these rocks into your backpack and you continue to add more rocks until you are so burdened by your load you get back and neck issues and can't go any farther! Meditation and mindfulness practices help you to sit down, take a breather, and put the backpack down for a moment. You can then begin the process of lightening your load and taking out some of the rocks that have been weighing you down.

When associations are built in the mind, a stimulus is connected to a thought and the neurons physically connect. If one neuron fires, the other automatically fires also. The result is additional stimuli repeating the thoughts of self-defeat and fear. While a single thought does not affect the mind or brain, the repetition of these thoughts can result in conditioning the brain to think and react in a certain manner that can eventually dominate our minds and lives. My scuba moment was a pivotal part of my journey toward liberating myself from my own internal negative narrative and moving toward more self-love and self-acceptance through the practice of mindfulness and the power of my breath.

The journey toward self-love and self-acceptance is not an easy one and probably why the word "journey" is used frequently, as it really is one! Through evolution, our brains are tiered toward a negativity bias, making us constantly scan for threats whether we are aware of it or not. This outlook served us in our cave-dwelling days but is no longer of that much use. It now causes our brains to be overactive, interpreting mildly stressful situations as code red emergencies. Constantly living in this state of heightened stress and anxiety over time causes us to become more prone to illness and disease.

Worrying Is a Waste of Time

It truly surprised me when I found out that the brain is unable to differentiate between something negative that is actually happening or something negative that we perceive to be happening. In a nutshell, when we worry or ruminate constantly about something that we are concerned or anxious about, it has the same impact on the physical body as if this situation is actually occurring versus just thinking about it happening.

I have learned over the years through my own meditation and mindfulness practice that worrying is a completely useless thing to do, as it never solves anything. Instead, it simply serves to heighten stress and anxiety related to whatever is causing the worry. There is an ancient Buddhist proverb that says worrying is the worst form of laziness as it corrupts you and takes your power away disabling you internally, and I could not agree more!

Negative experiences in our lives create the cycle of becoming over reactive and pessimistic and allowing more negative self-talk in our minds. This leaves us feeling dejected, sad, and anxious about the future. So what can you do about it? Well, you can use your mind to change your brain; the wallpaper of your mind, as I keep saying, becomes the landscape of your life. The thoughts that you have again and again create neural pathways in your brain so you tend to have similar reactions to things depending on these pathways that you create in your brain.

How you focus your attention and direct the flow of energy and information through your neural circuits can directly alter your brain's activity and structure. That is great if you are frequently having only good thoughts. For most of us, though, it tends to be more of that negative narrative that we keep playing over and over again in our minds. This in turn creates the internal circuitry in your brain that directly impacts how you react to things and how you live your daily life.

The Eternal Witness

The process of becoming a silent, impartial observer of the mind covered in a previous chapter is learning to become the witness,or *sakshi* as we call it in Sanskrit and yoga philosophy. So often we are completely unaware of our own thoughts, and our thoughts do not match up with our words and actions. We may be trying to live up to a certain ideal of ourselves or someone else's expectations of who we should be and how we should be living our lives. I am sure we can all think of people in our lives, ourselves included, whose words are not translating into their actions. This can leave us with a feeling of shame and guilt that we are not living up to either our own or other's expectations of how we should be living our lives, fueling the cycle of negative thinking.

Patanjali's *Yoga Sutra* mentions a concept called *pratipaksha bhavana,* a Sanskrit term that refers to thinking positive thoughts when disturbed by negative thoughts as an antidote to help calm the mind and bring it back into balance. Using this method will make the process of controlling the mind easier. It may sound overly simplistic, but often the most profound wisdom is!

The more frequently pratipaksha bhavana is practiced, the easier it becomes, but the most difficult part may be practicing consistently. Every time a negative thought comes up, think a positive one. I can guarantee that the more you do it, the more natural a process it becomes until it really becomes ingrained in you. You become so vigilant about the thoughts you are having that you no longer allow those habitual negative seeds to be planted in your mind because as soon as a negative thought arises, you are successfully able to redirect it.

Alongside this, my other pearl of wisdom, and what is equally as important, is to change your environment, as a negative environment further fuels negative thoughts. The older I get, I realize and embrace this truth wholeheartedly and encourage you to do the same. The company we keep is just as important as the thoughts we have in our minds.

No matter how positive your outlook is, unless you have extraordinary internal strength as Swami Satchidananda says, it is easy to become deflated by those around us and allow them to drag us down. Energy is contagious, positive and negative alike. I will forever be mindful of what and whom I allow in my space and life. I have a small very close circle of friends and that is enough for me. I know that these people are there when the times are tough but equally joyous and elated when things are going well.

Finding that balance is difficult the older you get in life, as people often project their own issues onto you consciously or unconsciously. Sometimes you may find that friends or family are finding it difficult to celebrate your success if they feel they are not where they want to be in life, which is understandable. We can certainly send these people love, compassion, and good wishes but it certainly does not mean that we need to take on their baggage and issues. Trust me on this one! You cannot surround yourself with negative people and expect to live a positive life and that is the truth.

Bad Attitudes Block Miracles

A bad attitude can block love, miracles, and blessings from manifesting in your life. Don't be the reason you don't succeed because you are unable to control your thoughts and are not consciously choosing to surround yourself with people who are serving your highest good. It is only when you are aware and present in each and every moment that you begin to be able to observe the internal dialogue going on within your own mind. This is all that you actually have control over anyway.

When you become truly aware of your innermost thoughts that result in the conditioning of your mind, you are able to change your patterns of thinking from negative to positive. You are as a result better equipped to alter your external environment from negative to positive. Meditation is a scientifically proven method of being able to change the way you think and it actually works, if you do it. The next time someone tells you that change is not possible, just ignore them and instead go to your place of peace and quiet within where you know anything is possible. Don't base your decisions on the advice of those who don't have to deal with the results.

You deal with the consequences of your decisions, so learn to be led from within. As covered earlier in the book, everybody will always have an opinion on what you should do and how you should live your life. Mindfulness and meditation allow you to be able to tune in and start to drown out the negative chatter and turn the volume up on the positive thoughts, as those are the ones you want to amplify. Our exercise for this chapter guides you in starting to notice your thoughts and begin the process of replacing your negative thoughts with more positive ones.

Self-Love and the Power of Sleep

Another wonderful benefit of a meditation practice is that you will sleep better, which helps with our mood. Good sleep helps with hormone regulation and contributes to alleviating stress and anxiety in the body and mind. If you are one of those people who have no issues with sleep whatsoever and as soon as your head hits the pillow you are off in a deep slumber, you are very fortunate.

Unfortunately, many people find it difficult to fall or stay asleep. Between fifty to seventy million Americans suffer from a sleep disorder so much so that it has become a national public health crisis. Insufficient sleep has been linked to car accidents and chronic diseases ranging from diabetes to depression. So many people are looking for ways to help calm their over stimulated minds in time for bed so they can get the much needed rest the body needs in order to rejuvenate from within.

The quality of your sleep is just as important as the hours spent with your head on your pillow. Interrupted sleep can rob you of more of the deep restorative sleep that is necessary for your health and well-being. I can tell you as the mother to a baby who has not slept properly since he was born, consistently interrupted sleep will drive you to the brink of insanity, especially when you throw in a screaming baby! I would truly have lost it without my yoga and meditation practice and credit these two things with keeping me sane and stable.

Simple things that you can start doing to aid in getting a better night's rest include practicing some breath work before bed to help clear your mind. Simply take a few deep inhales and exhales a number of times, visualizing yourself emptying your mind of the day's events. Set a consistent bedtime, and avoid consuming too much caffeine or alcohol leading up to bedtime. If you also end up waking up to go to the bathroom during the night, try to limit your intake of fluids a minimum of an hour before bed. I swear by blackout shades in the bedroom that help block light in the room, and cannot sleep without my eye mask that helps to create that sense of darkness in the room, night or day.

Use mood lighting in your house as evening commences, dimming lights before bed and creating a calm, soothing environment in your house and bedroom. Burning essential oils can be very helpful and some of my favorite ones for bed are lavender, ylang-ylang, and sandalwood. These are a few of my top picks and ones that I use in our home to aid relaxation and get those bedtime vibes going.

Another tip is to limit the use of electronics at least thirty minutes but ideally an hour before bed and to use blue light blockers on your devices. Blue light from device screens inhibits the production of melatonin, the hormone that regulates sleep cycles. It has been found that exposure to blue light suppresses melatonin production.

Meditation will help you lead a happier, more fulfilled life with better sleep. I guarantee it! If you don't believe me, ask anyone who has a consistent daily meditation practice if they feel as though their life has changed for the better because of meditation; hear their journey for yourself. Every single person I have ever met who meditates regularly vouches for the life transformational benefits a regular practice has offered them. So much so that now they cannot live without meditation; it has become just as much a part of their day and life as brushing their teeth, showering, or eating. Our exercise for this chapter helps you to activate the *ajna* or third eye chakra to create greater harmony and balance in your daily life.

Exercise

Five-Minute Self-Love Meditation

Begin by taking at least three deep inhales through the nose and exhales out the mouth. Then return to your normal rhythm and pattern of breathing, and bring your attention and focus to the point between your eyebrows, the ajna or third eye chakra, the seat of your highest intuition and inner wisdom. This is the sixth chakra of the seven chakras or energy centers in the body located along the spine. Start to visualize a vibrant light purple color in this area and repeat the mantra "I love and accept myself" three times. Then sit in silence, allowing your mind to come to that place of stillness and quiet from within. Tuning in to your inner wisdom is pivotal in order to guide you on the path toward greater self-love and self-acceptance.

Conclusion

"The proof is in the pudding" is a very popular saying in England where I am from, possibly because we love puddings! Meditation works, but you have to do it and you have to do it daily. Like anything in life, it will not work if you don't do it. We can shy away from anything that requires real work and effort on our part but this path never yields great results.

Everything good I have achieved in my life has come from hard work, dedication, and an unrelenting commitment to further myself in a positive way on my journey in life. The more you meditate, the more you will see your life transform for the better. I see it in my own life and the lives of my patients and clients all the time. This transformation is what keeps us coming back to the practice day in and day out.

I want to share the story of one of my clients who, when I started working with her, had never meditated before. She came to me in crisis, overwhelmed by the negativity in her relationship with her partner with whom she had been deeply unhappy for some time. Not really finding fulfillment from working from home she also wanted to find a job that allowed her to be in a workplace around people who were uplifting and in a job where she was valued and felt rewarded for her efforts. She was also experiencing difficulty with her son and the lack of respect he was continually showing to her.

My client began a daily meditation practice and stuck to it; without fail, she completed her morning five-minute meditation and most days also completed the evening meditation. This was a total of only twelve minutes for both meditations each day. Talk about meditation working! Within three months she had split up with her partner and moved on from that very toxic relationship and recognized her habitual negative thought patterns that kept her locked in a cycle of always attracting the wrong man. She found a new job in a wonderful company and her relationship with her son has improved dramatically. Most importantly, she is working on rebuilding herself after years of being in physically and emotionally abusive relationships.

Her goal through her meditation practice is greater self-love, self-acceptance, and self-empowerment. That is the power of meditation, it can and will change your life and only for the better. Now six months into her practice, she notices the difference in her mind and body if she skips a day, and it is what keeps her focused on committing to a daily practice. I have countless other stories of clients who began a meditation practice and they experienced a complete and total one-hundred-eighty-degree life transformation. I will leave you with the tools outlined in this book so you too can experience a change from within, to transform your life through the power of meditation and mindfulness.

From the bottom of my heart, I wish you the very best on your path forward with these practices. If you are able to commit to a daily five-minute meditation practice and make use of the intentions and five-minute exercises in this book, I have no doubts that you will start to see a difference in your mind and life. As I like to say and have said repeatedly, the wallpaper of your mind becomes the landscape of your life. Choose your wallpaper wisely and make sure that your thoughts are serving you to be the best version of yourself each day, creating lasting peace and happiness from within. You deserve it!

Resources

For more information on my meditation and spiritual life coaching program, please visit www.shantiwithin.com/shop where you can sign up to my intention-based meditation and coaching program and start meditating your way to a new you. You can also access a free meditation via this link that will aid you in becoming calmer and more balanced, which helps in every aspect of your life from manifesting the things you deeply desire to getting a good night's rest.

Acknowledgments

A special thank you to the amazing Dr. Allyson Brooks, MD, FACOG, executive medical director Women's Health Institute; vice president Performance Improvement; and Ginny Ueberroth, Endowed Chair, Hoag Hospital who I have been blessed to have as a mentor, colleague and friend long my journey. Dr. Brooks is a shining example of an empowered woman who truly inspires and empowers other women.

I also want to thank another dear friend and colleague Dr. Heather Macdonald, MD, FACOG, medical director, Hoag Hospital Breast and Ovarian Cancer Prevention program who secured the funding and worked tirelessly with me over the past few years to create the Feasibility Study to explore perioperative pain management for breast cancer patients through meditation and pranayama practices.

A heartfelt thank you to my dear friend and colleague Dr. Sadia Khan, DO, FACS, FACOS, director, Integrative Breast Oncology at Hoag Hospital and assistant clinical professor of surgery, Keck School of Medicine USC, and Kerstin Gulden, one of my closest friends for providing me with invaluable feedback as I wrote this book.

A huge thank you to Anne Rierson at Aura Cacia and Deb Foley from San Clemente Web Design. These two amazing women were complete strangers, yet so supportive from the very beginning of my journey with my business. I am forever grateful to them for helping me along my path and supporting my work.

Special thank you to one of my oldest friends, Amber Dreadon, for believing in me and my vision and being the producer and director for my Minute Mindfulness series, so grateful for your friendship and support.

A big thank you to my Mum, Dad, sister Sharmila, family and friends, especially my London crew to name but a few who I refer to in this book: Panyin, Nikki, Roli, Yvette, Emily, Helen, Mary, Veronica, Sheryl, and Ainsley for your ongoing unconditional love and support. Finally, I have saved the best for last: a *huge* thank you to my amazing husband, James Tokumoto, for always believing in me even when I doubted myself. I am so grateful for our life together with our sweet son, Suriya, the light of my life, and our adorable four-legged son, Benson.

To Write to the Author

If you wish to contact the author or would like more information about this book, please write to the author in care of Llewellyn Worldwide Ltd. and we will forward your request. Both the author and publisher appreciate hearing from you and learning of your enjoyment of this book and how it has helped you. Llewellyn Worldwide Ltd. cannot guarantee that every letter written to the author can be answered, but all will be forwarded. Please write to:

Anusha Wijeyakumar MA
c/o Llewellyn Worldwide
2143 Wooddale Drive
Woodbury, MN 55125-2989

Please enclose a self-addressed stamped envelope for reply, or $1.00 to cover costs. If outside the U.S.A., enclose an international postal reply coupon.

Many of Llewellyn's authors have websites with additional information and resources. For more information, please visit our website at http://www.llewellyn.com.